THE GOLDEN BOOK OF

FACTS
AND
FIGURES

A Treasury of Information on Hundreds of Subjects

With More than 500 Pictures in Color

BY **BERTHA MORRIS PARKER**

Formerly of the Laboratory Schools, University of Chicago
Research Associate, Chicago Natural History Museum

DESIGNED AND ILLUSTRATED BY **LOWELL HESS**

 GOLDEN PRESS · NEW YORK

CONTENTS

ACKNOWLEDGMENTS

Page 4, lower right: The Metropolitan Museum of Art, Rogers Fund, 1926–1931

Pages 24–25, 29: All photographs Mt. Wilson and Palomar Observatories except Great Nebula in Orion: Clarence P. Custer, M.D.

Some of the illustrations in this book were done by the following artists: Mel T. Crawford, James Gordon Irving, Harry McNaught, and Gregory Orlorff.

Library of Congress Catalog Card Number: 62-15854

1 MCLX

PYTHAGORAS

THE ROUTE OF THE "VICTORIA"

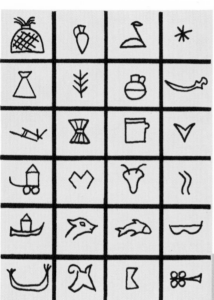

ANCIENT SUMERIAN SCRIPT

ANCIENT MAP OF NIPPUR

SPHINX WITH HEAD OF QUEEN HAT-SHEPSUT

MONTGOLFIER BALLOON

FIFTY FIRSTS

The first paintings we know about were done on the walls of caves in southern Europe about 20,000 B.C.

The earliest doctor to have his name come down to us was an Egyptian, I-am-hotep, said to have lived as long ago as 4500 B.C.

The first written language known is Sumerian, dating back to 3100 B.C.

The first medical prescriptions we know about were those of Dr. Lulu of Ur, who practiced about 2700 B.C.

By 2700 B.C. the Egyptians had the world's first solar calendar, with a year of 365 days.

The first known code of laws dates from about 2050 B.C. It is the Ur-Nammu code. This collection of laws is about 300 years older than the famous code of Hammurabi.

The first recorded murder trial took place in Sumer about 1850 B.C. One archeologist has called it "The Case of the Silent Wife."

The first "farmer's almanac" was written in Sumer about 1700 B.C.

The first alphabet is believed to have been invented by some of the Semitic peoples at the eastern end of the Mediterranean Sea about 1500 B.C.

The earliest map ever found is one of the city of Nippur, drawn about 1500 B.C. It shows clearly the buildings, rivers, canals, walls, and gates of Nippur as well as its "Central Park."

The first known manual on the care of horses was written in Sumerian some 3400 years ago. It was found in Turkey.

The first great woman recorded in history was Queen Hat-shepsut of Egypt. Her reign was approximately from 1485–1468 B.C.

The earliest shipwrecked vessel to have its treasure found at the bottom of the sea was wrecked on an island off the coast of what is now Turkey about 1400 B.C.

The first Olympic Games of which there is a record were held in 776 B.C. They were held just outside the small town of Olympia in Greece and consisted only of a foot race of about 200 yards. The first modern Olympic Games were held in Athens in 1896 with nine nations competing.

Pythagoras of Greece (580?–500? B.C.) was the first person to claim that the earth is round.

Democritus of Greece (460?–362? B.C.) was the first person to suggest that the Milky Way is composed of a vast number of faint stars.

Aristarchus of Samos (310?–230? B.C.) was the first person to state the belief that the earth travels around the sun and that the moon travels around the earth.

Eratosthenes (276–194 B.C.) was the first to work out the circumference of the earth at the equator. He was so good a geographer and mathematician that he was only 238 miles off.

The first printed book we know about was made in China in 848 by Wang Chieh. He carved each page in a block of wood. Printing with movable type came considerably later: printing with porcelain type about 900 years ago in China, and printing with metal type some 500 years later in Germany.

The first ship to sail around the world was the Spanish ship "Victoria." Commanded on the first half of the voyage by Magellan and, after his death, by Sebastian del Cano, it left Spain on Sept. 20, 1519, and did not return until Sept. 6, 1522.

The first printing press in the New World was set up in Mexico City in 1536.

The first city in what is now the United States was St. Augustine, Fla., settled in 1565.

The first yacht race on record was one held in England in 1662. One of the sailors was the English king, Charles II. The royal yacht won.

The first American circulating library was started in Philadelphia in 1731.

The first successful balloon was designed by the Montgolfier brothers and was launched in France on June 5, 1783. The first manned flight was made in a similar balloon on Nov. 21, 1783.

The first state to ratify the Constitution of the United States was Delaware. It ratified the Constitution on Dec. 7, 1789.

Andre-Jacques Garnerin made the first parachute jump in Paris on Oct. 22, 1797, from a height of about 6,500 feet.

Oberlin College, at Oberlin, Ohio, was the first coeducational college in the United States. It was founded in 1833.

The first baseball game, as we know the game today, was played in Hoboken, N.J., on June 19, 1846, between the Knickerbockers and the New York Nine.

The first woman doctor in the United States was Elizabeth Blackwell. She received her M.D. degree from Geneva Medical College of Western New York in 1849.

The first commercial oil well in the United States was drilled in Titusville, Pa., in 1859.

The first curve balls in baseball were pitched by "Candy" Cummings in 1867.

In 1869 the Cincinnati Red Stockings, the first all-professional baseball team, played 64 games without a loss.

The first formal intercollegiate "football" game was played Nov. 6, 1869, at New Brunswick, N.J., between Princeton and Rutgers. It was really soccer.

Mrs. Adah H. Kepley was the first woman to receive a law degree in the United States. She received her degree from the Union College of Law in Chicago in 1870.

The first "5 and 10" was founded by Frank Woolworth in Utica, N.Y., in 1879.

The first building to be called a skyscraper, the Home Insurance Company building in Chicago, was built in 1885.

"The Yellow Kid" by Richard Outcault was the first colored cartoon. It appeared in 1895 in the *New York World*.

Orville Wright made the first successful airplane flight at Kitty Hawk, N.C., on Dec. 17, 1903.

The North Pole was first reached by Commodore Robert E. Peary and his party of five on April 6, 1909.

The South Pole was first reached on Dec. 14, 1911, by Roald Amundsen.

On Dec. 2, 1942, the first controlled nuclear chain reaction was achieved by Enrico Fermi at the University of Chicago.

The highest point on earth, the top of Mount Everest, was first reached on May 29, 1953, by Sir Edmund Hillary and Tensing Norkay.

On May 6, 1954, Roger Bannister of England became the first man to run a mile in less than 4 minutes. His time was 3 min., 59.4 sec.

The "Nautilus," launched Jan. 21, 1954, at Groton, Conn., was the first atomic submarine. The first atomic merchant ship, the N.S. "Savannah," was launched July 21, 1959, at Camden, N.J. "N.S." stands for "Nuclear Ship."

Don Larsen of the New York Yankees pitched the first perfect game in a World Series on Oct. 8, 1956.

The world's first atomic power station for producing electricity for civilian use began operation on Oct. 17, 1956, at Calder Hill in England.

The first nonstop, round-the-world jet plane flight was completed on Jan. 18, 1957, by three United States Air Force bombers under the command of Major General Archie J. Old. The flight took 45 hours and 19 minutes.

The first man-made earth satellite, Sputnik I, was launched on Oct. 4, 1957.

The first artificial planet, Lunik I, was shot into space on Jan. 2, 1959.

THE "NAUTILUS"

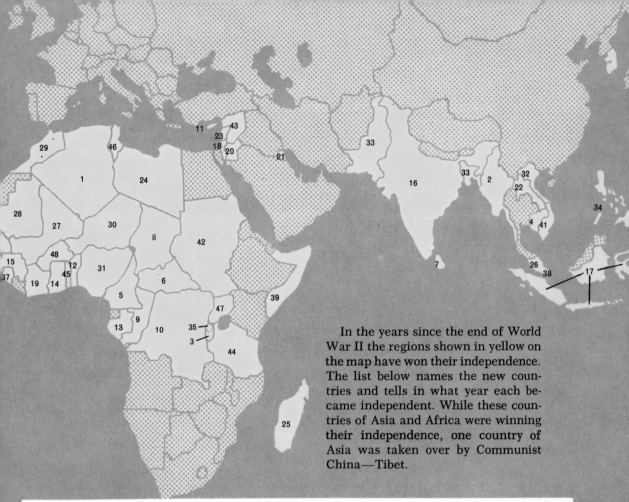

In the years since the end of World War II the regions shown in yellow on the map have won their independence. The list below names the new countries and tells in what year each became independent. While these countries of Asia and Africa were winning their independence, one country of Asia was taken over by Communist China—Tibet.

THE MARCH TO INDEPENDENCE IN ASIA AND AFRICA

KEY	COUNTRY	YEAR	KEY	COUNTRY	YEAR
1	Algeria	1962	26	Malaya	1957
2	Burma	1948	27	Mali	1960
3	Burundi	1962	28	Mauritania	1960
4	Cambodia	1955	29	Morocco	1956
5	Cameroun	1960	30	Niger	1960
6	Central African Republic	1960	31	Nigeria	1960
7	Ceylon	1948	32	North Vietnam	1954
8	Chad	1960	33	Pakistan	1947
9	Congo (formerly French)	1960	34	Philippines	1946
10	Congo (formerly Belgian)	1960	35	Rwanda	1962
11	Cyprus	1959	36	Senegal	1960
12	Dahomey	1960	37	Sierra Leone	1961
13	Gabon	1960	38	Singapore State	1958
14	Ghana	1957	39	Somalia	1960
15	Guinea	1958	40	South Korea	1948
16	India	1947	41	South Vietnam	1954
17	Indonesia	1949	42	Sudan	1956
18	Israel	1948	43	Syria	1944
19	Ivory Coast	1960	44	Tanganyika	1961
20	Jordan	1946	45	Togo	1960
21	Kuwait	1961	46	Tunisia	1956
22	Laos	1949	47	Uganda	1962
23	Lebanon	1941	48	Upper Volta	1960
24	Libya	1951		Western Samoa	1962
25	Malagasy (Madagascar)	1960		(not shown on map)	

THE FIFTY UNITED STATES

Can you identify the various states from their shapes and comparative sizes?

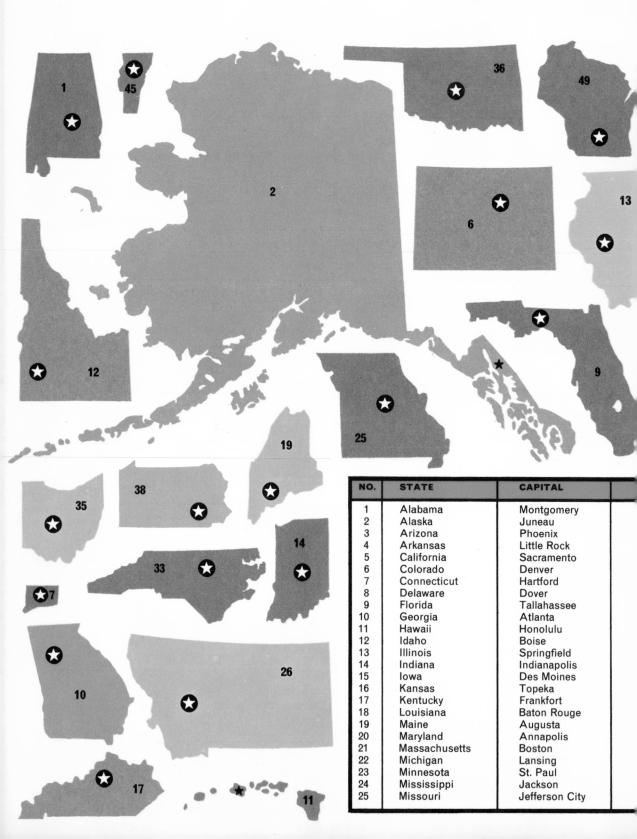

NO.	STATE	CAPITAL	
1	Alabama	Montgomery	
2	Alaska	Juneau	
3	Arizona	Phoenix	
4	Arkansas	Little Rock	
5	California	Sacramento	
6	Colorado	Denver	
7	Connecticut	Hartford	
8	Delaware	Dover	
9	Florida	Tallahassee	
10	Georgia	Atlanta	
11	Hawaii	Honolulu	
12	Idaho	Boise	
13	Illinois	Springfield	
14	Indiana	Indianapolis	
15	Iowa	Des Moines	
16	Kansas	Topeka	
17	Kentucky	Frankfort	
18	Louisiana	Baton Rouge	
19	Maine	Augusta	
20	Maryland	Annapolis	
21	Massachusetts	Boston	
22	Michigan	Lansing	
23	Minnesota	St. Paul	
24	Mississippi	Jackson	
25	Missouri	Jefferson City	

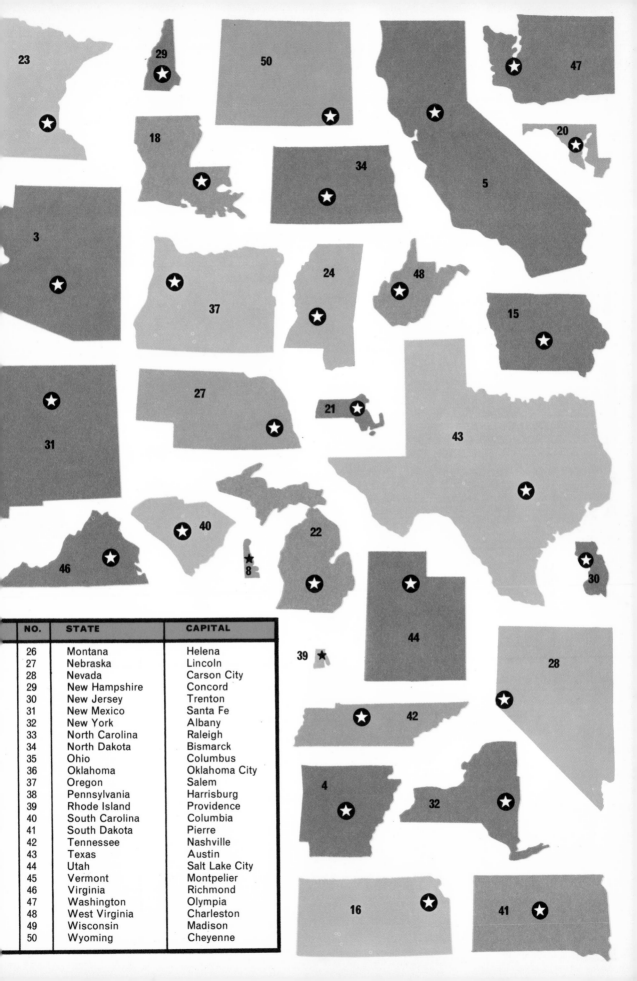

NO.	STATE	CAPITAL
26	Montana	Helena
27	Nebraska	Lincoln
28	Nevada	Carson City
29	New Hampshire	Concord
30	New Jersey	Trenton
31	New Mexico	Santa Fe
32	New York	Albany
33	North Carolina	Raleigh
34	North Dakota	Bismarck
35	Ohio	Columbus
36	Oklahoma	Oklahoma City
37	Oregon	Salem
38	Pennsylvania	Harrisburg
39	Rhode Island	Providence
40	South Carolina	Columbia
41	South Dakota	Pierre
42	Tennessee	Nashville
43	Texas	Austin
44	Utah	Salt Lake City
45	Vermont	Montpelier
46	Virginia	Richmond
47	Washington	Olympia
48	West Virginia	Charleston
49	Wisconsin	Madison
50	Wyoming	Cheyenne

FAMOUS HOAXES

A hoax is an object or a story meant to deceive people. It may not be recognized as a hoax for years. There have been a great many famous hoaxes. Here are a few of them.

THE WILD ANIMAL HOAX

In the *New York Herald* of November 9, 1874, big headlines and an article which took up several columns told about the escape of all the animals in the Central Park Zoo. Twenty-seven people who had been killed were named, and two hundred others were said to be injured. Chester A. Arthur was mentioned as one of the well-known New Yorkers who had taken part in the animal hunt. Everyone was urged to stay indoors until the twelve animals still at large were tracked down and captured.

Actually a paragraph at the end of the story told that it had been made up to call attention to some of the shortcomings of the zoo. But not many readers read that paragraph. One editor of another newspaper, the *Times,* made a trip to the New York City police headquarters to ask why a rival newspaper had been given this scoop.

FEEJEE MERMAID

P. T. Barnum was famous for hoaxes. He was convinced that the public enjoyed being fooled. One of his best-known hoaxes was the Feejee Mermaid. Posters advertising it showed a beautiful mermaid swimming about in water. What the people who paid to look at the mermaid saw was the stuffed head of a monkey sewed to the stuffed body and tail of a large fish.

THE LOST DAUPHIN

In an article in the February, 1853, number of *Putnam's Monthly*, Eleazar Williams claimed that he was Louis XVII of France, the son of Louis XVI and Marie Antoinette. Louis XVII is often called the "lost dauphin." During the French Revolution the dauphin, a young boy, was put in prison. Later he was said to have died there. But there were rumors that he had been rescued. At one time 27 different people claimed to be the lost prince.

Eleazar Williams, supposedly the son of an American Indian father, claimed that 11 years before he wrote the article an emissary had come from Louis Philippe, who was then king of France, and had asked him to sign away all his rights to the throne of France. Until that time Williams had not known who he was. No one could be found to back up his claims. But the people of Hogansburg, New York, and Green Bay, Wisconsin, two places where Williams lived at different times, kept alive the story that he was the lost dauphin.

To end such stories, the Paris Court of Appeals in 1954 declared that the real dauphin had died in prison when he was ten.

CARDIFF GIANT

In 1889 William C. Newell, a farmer who lived near Cardiff, New York, hired some of his neighbors to help him dig a well. When they had dug down five feet they came to what seemed to be a petrified giant. The figure was 12 feet long and 5 feet broad. Its legs were slightly drawn up as if the giant had been in great pain just before he died. Within 24 hours a tent had been set up over the "giant" and people were paying admission to see it. An Indian squaw was sure the giant was an Indian chief of her tribe, one who had said that he would be seen again. Some of the viewers, however, thought that the giant was a hoax, and it turned out to be.

A relative of Mr. Newell's had hired a stonecutter to carve the statue. It cost several thousand dollars. Then the statue had had holes made in it with darning needles, had been scrubbed with sand, and had been bathed in sulfuric acid to make it look ancient. The idea was partly to make money by showing it and partly to win an argument as to whether there had been giants in early times.

HI-BRAZIL

In the time of Columbus, and for at least 350 years afterward, maps of the North Atlantic showed a small island named Hi-Brazil southwest of Ireland. A number of mariners reported sailing close to it, and in September,

1674, a Captain John Nisbet reported having actually landed on it. When he made his report he had with him a group of Scotsmen whom he said he had rescued from the island. Hi-Brazil, he told, was inhabited chiefly by huge black rabbits, but the ruler was a wicked magician. The magician had cast a spell over the Scotsmen, who had been shipwrecked on the island. Captain Nisbet had broken the spell by building a bonfire on the shore and had been able to rescue the captives. Mapmakers of today are sure that there never was a Hi-Brazil.

SERPENT OF LOCH NESS

In 1911 stories of a terrible sea serpent in Loch Ness in the Scottish highlands drew many tourists to the region to see the monster. For years from then on people reported seeing it. Some said it was 30 feet long; some said 300. "Nessie" and "Loopie" were two of its nicknames. A retired commander in the British Navy asked Parliament to protect the monster with a special act. At last a group of scientists was organized to make an investigation. Their conclusion, in spite of stories of eye witnesses and of some indistinct pictures, was that there was no such monster.

THE POEMS OF BILITIS

Late in the 19th century the *Poems of Bilitis* were "discovered." Bilitis was said to be a Greek poetess who had lived in the 6th century B.C. Her house, the story went, had been torn down, and its stones had been used to pave the quays of Port Said. She was buried beside an ancient road. The poems were supposedly found in a Phoenician tomb.

Many scholars accepted the poems as genuine. Nearly a hundred were translated into other languages. The famous Claude Debussy set four of them to music.

The poems were beautiful, but they were written by a young Frenchman, Pierre Louÿs. He and a classmate planned the hoax because they were angry at the way some of the scholars of other lands looked down on French writers of the time.

PILTDOWN MAN

In 1911 Charles Dawson dug up a jawbone and the top of a skull in a gravel pit in southern England. He convinced scientists who saw them that they were bones of a type of prehistoric man not known before. This prehistoric man was named the Piltdown man and was thought to date back 500,000 years. In 1953, long after Dawson had died, the find was proved to be a hoax. The jawbone was the jaw of a modern ape cleverly treated to make it appear old, and the top of the skull, which was actually a person's skull, was 50,000 rather than 500,000 years old.

AN "ENIGMATICAL PROPHECY"

In *Poor Richard's Almanac* for 1736 Benjamin Franklin put this prophecy: Many of America's cities would soon be under water, a power with which the Colonies were not at war would drive many ships out of their ports, and an army would land and annoy the Colonists. In the *Almanac* for 1737 Franklin explained that his prophecy had come to pass. Many American cities had been covered with water because clouds are made of drops of water, the power that drove the ships away from the ports was the wind, and the army that landed was an army of mosquitoes.

THE MOON HOAX

In August of 1935 a series of articles appeared in the *New York Sun* which boosted the *Sun's* circulation till it was the largest of any newspaper in the world. The articles were about life on the moon. Through a big new telescope in South Africa, they said, the English astronomer Sir John Herschel had seen on the moon bison, goats, big birds such as cranes and pelicans, and, most exciting of all, furry, winged men. These men, according to the stories, were about four feet tall and, except for their faces, were covered with copper-colored hair. They kept their big wings folded as they walked about. Richard Adams Locke, one of the *Sun's* writers, finally admitted that he had made up the stories just to win new readers for the paper.

FOREIGN EXPRESSIONS

à cheval (Fr.), on horseback.

affaire d'honneur (Fr.), a duel.

aloha (Hawaiian), greetings; farewell.

así, así (Sp.), so-so.

autre temps, autres moeurs (Fr.), other times, other customs.

beaux-arts (Fr.), fine arts.

bon marché (Fr.), a bargain.

bon vivant (Fr.), an epicure.

bon voyage (Fr.), a good journey (to you).

caen chuzos de punta (Sp.), it's raining cats and dogs.

cause célèbre (Fr.), a famous (legal) case.

cave canem (Lat.), beware (of) the dog.

caveat emptor (Lat.), let the buyer beware.

cead míle fáilte (Irish), a hundred thousand welcomes.

c'est la guerre (Fr.), it is war.

chacun à son goût (Fr.), each to his taste.

cherchez la femme (Fr.), look for the woman (back of this).

comme il faut (Fr.), as it should be.

corpus delicti (Lat.), the body (basic facts) of the crime.

coup d'état (Fr.), an unexpected show of force or authority.

cum grano salis (Lat.), with a grain of salt.

Deo gratias (Lat.), thanks be to God.

de profundis (Lat.), out of the depths.

de rigueur (Fr.), according to strict etiquette.

dernier cri (Fr.), the newest fashion.

de trop (Fr.), too many, superfluous.

el tiempo es oro (Sp.), time is money.

entre nous (Fr.), between us; confidentially.

erase una vez (Sp.), once upon a time.

esprit de corps (Fr.), group spirit.

ex libris (Lat.), from the books (of).

faux pas (Fr.), a social blunder.

gesundheit (Ger.), (to your) health.

hacer castillos en el aire (Sp.), to build castles in the air.

hoi polloi (Greek), the common people.

ideé fixe (Fr.), a fixed idea.

in excelsis (Lat.), in the highest.

in loco parentis (Lat.), in place of a parent.

inshallah (Arabic), God willing.

joie de vivre (Fr.), joy of living.

kamaaina (Hawaiian), "old-timer."

laissez faire (Fr.), noninterference.

magna cum laude (Lat.), with great praise.

mal de mer (Fr.), seasickness.

malihini (Hawaiian), newcomer.

mirabile dictu (Lat.), wonderful to tell.

noblesse oblige (Fr.), nobility obligates (certain behavior).

objet d'art (Fr.), a work of art.

pax vobiscum (Lat.), peace be with you.

persona non grata (Lat.), a person who is not acceptable.

poco a poco (It. and Sp.), little by little.

ENGLISH	FRENCH	GERMAN	ITALIAN	SPANISH	SWEDISH
Good morning	Bon jour	Guten Morgen	Buon giorno	Buenos dias	God morgon
Merry Christmas	Joyeux Noël	Fröhliche Weih-nachten	Buon Natale	Felices Pascuas	God Jul
Please	S'il vous plaît	Bitte	Per favore	Por favor	Var snäll och
Thank you	Merci beaucoup	Danke schön	Grazie	Muchas gracias	Tack så mycket
You are welcome	Il n'y pas de quoi	Bitte	Prego	De nada	Var så god
Yes	Oui	Ja	Si	Si	Ja
No	Non	Nein	No	No	Nej
Good-bye	Au revoir	Auf Wiedersehen	Addio	Adios	Adjö

post bellum (Lat.), after the war.
pro patria (Lat.), for one's country.
que sera sera (Sp.), what will be will be.
¿quien sabe? (Sp.), who knows?
raison d'être (Fr.), reason for being.
rara avis (Lat.), someone or something out of the ordinary ("rare bird").
répondez s'il vous plaît (Fr.), answer if you please. (R.S.V.P.).
sans souci (Fr.), without worry.
savoir-faire (Fr.), knowledge of how to act.
semper fidelis (Lat.), always faithful.
soy todo oidos (Sp.), I am all ears.
status quo (Lat.), the present situation.
tempus fugit (Lat.), time flies.
tout ensemble (Fr.), all together.
una vida de perros (Sp.), a dog's life.

FORMERLY FOREIGN, NOW ENGLISH

ad infinitum (Lat.), without limit.
a la carte (Fr.), each dish priced separately.
a la mode (Fr.), fashionable.
alter ego (Lat.), second self; bosom friend.
anno Domini (Lat.), in the year of our Lord.
belles-lettres (Fr.), literature.
billet-doux (Fr.), a love letter or note.
bon mot (Fr.), witty saying.
et cetera (Lat.), and other things.
ex officio (Lat.), by virtue of his office.
finis (Lat.), the end.
magnum opus (Lat.), one's greatest work.
nom de plume (Fr.), pen name.
par excellence (Fr.), outstanding.
paterfamilias (Lat.), head of the household.
per se (Lat.), by itself.
sine die (Lat.), without a day set.
table d'hôte (Fr.), a meal for which one pays a fixed price.
tête-à-tête (Fr.), private conversation.
tour de force (Fr.), a feat of skill.

ENG	FR	GER	ITAL	SP	SWED	LATIN
one	un	eins	uno	uno	en	unus
two	deux	zwei	due	dos	två	duo
three	trois	drei	tre	tres	tre	tres
four	quatre	vier	quattro	cuatro	fyra	quattuor
five	cinq	fünf	cinque	cinco	fem	quinque
six	six	sechs	sei	seis	sex	sex
seven	sept	sieben	sette	siete	sju	septem
eight	huit	acht	otto	ocho	åtta	octo
nine	neuf	neun	nove	nueve	nio	novem
ten	dix	zehn	dieci	diez	tio	decem

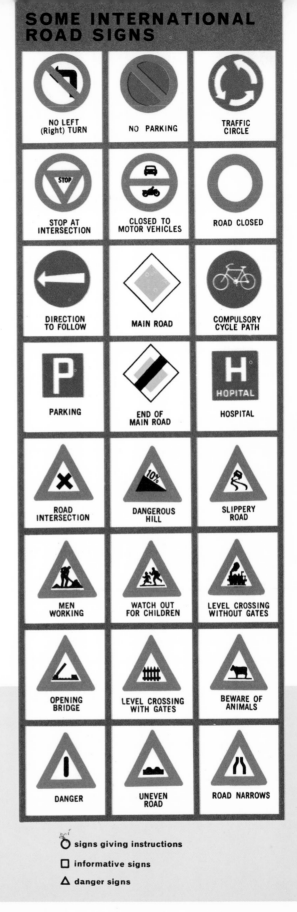

SOME INTERNATIONAL ROAD SIGNS

NO LEFT (Right) TURN — NO PARKING — TRAFFIC CIRCLE

STOP AT INTERSECTION — CLOSED TO MOTOR VEHICLES — ROAD CLOSED

DIRECTION TO FOLLOW — MAIN ROAD — COMPULSORY CYCLE PATH

PARKING — END OF MAIN ROAD — HOSPITAL

ROAD INTERSECTION — DANGEROUS HILL — SLIPPERY ROAD

MEN WORKING — WATCH OUT FOR CHILDREN — LEVEL CROSSING WITHOUT GATES

OPENING BRIDGE — LEVEL CROSSING WITH GATES — BEWARE OF ANIMALS

DANGER — UNEVEN ROAD — ROAD NARROWS

○ signs giving instructions

□ informative signs

△ danger signs

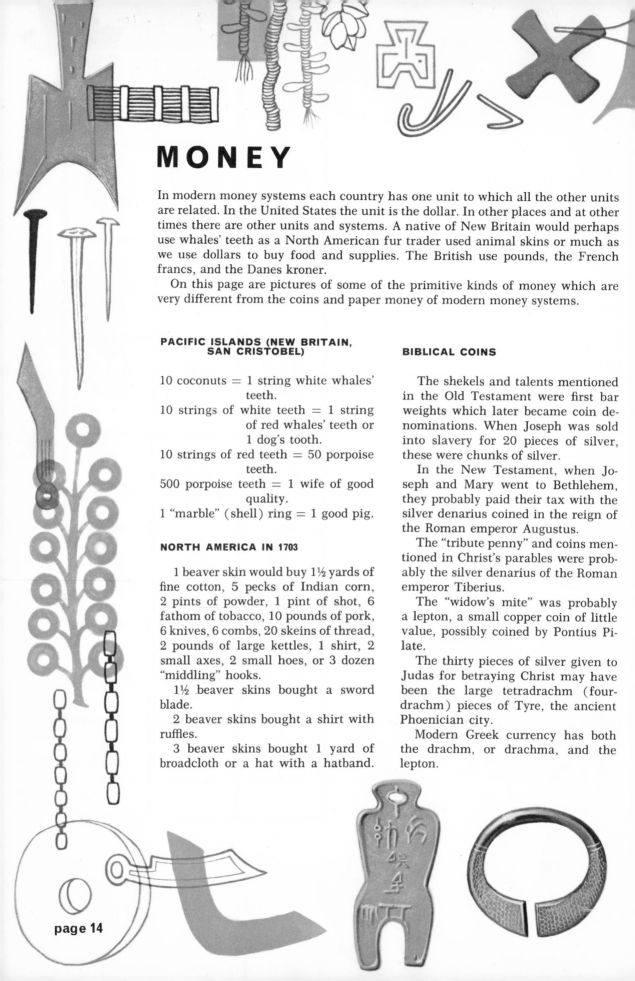

MONEY

In modern money systems each country has one unit to which all the other units are related. In the United States the unit is the dollar. In other places and at other times there are other units and systems. A native of New Britain would perhaps use whales' teeth as a North American fur trader used animal skins or much as we use dollars to buy food and supplies. The British use pounds, the French francs, and the Danes kroner.

On this page are pictures of some of the primitive kinds of money which are very different from the coins and paper money of modern money systems.

PACIFIC ISLANDS (NEW BRITAIN, SAN CRISTOBEL)

10 coconuts = 1 string white whales' teeth.

10 strings of white teeth = 1 string of red whales' teeth or 1 dog's tooth.

10 strings of red teeth = 50 porpoise teeth.

500 porpoise teeth = 1 wife of good quality.

1 "marble" (shell) ring = 1 good pig.

NORTH AMERICA IN 1703

1 beaver skin would buy 1½ yards of fine cotton, 5 pecks of Indian corn, 2 pints of powder, 1 pint of shot, 6 fathom of tobacco, 10 pounds of pork, 6 knives, 6 combs, 20 skeins of thread, 2 pounds of large kettles, 1 shirt, 2 small axes, 2 small hoes, or 3 dozen "middling" hooks.

1½ beaver skins bought a sword blade.

2 beaver skins bought a shirt with ruffles.

3 beaver skins bought 1 yard of broadcloth or a hat with a hatband.

BIBLICAL COINS

The shekels and talents mentioned in the Old Testament were first bar weights which later became coin denominations. When Joseph was sold into slavery for 20 pieces of silver, these were chunks of silver.

In the New Testament, when Joseph and Mary went to Bethlehem, they probably paid their tax with the silver denarius coined in the reign of the Roman emperor Augustus.

The "tribute penny" and coins mentioned in Christ's parables were probably the silver denarius of the Roman emperor Tiberius.

The "widow's mite" was probably a lepton, a small copper coin of little value, possibly coined by Pontius Pilate.

The thirty pieces of silver given to Judas for betraying Christ may have been the large tetradrachm (four-drachm) pieces of Tyre, the ancient Phoenician city.

Modern Greek currency has both the drachm, or drachma, and the lepton.

Many, many designs have been used on coins. Around this page are designs from coins of different places and times. Something important to the place or to its history, religion, or legends is usually represented. And often the design is quite beautiful.

Histories and stories mention the names of different kinds of money. The names can sometimes be traced back to ancient times when weights of metal or numbers of cattle or sheep were measures of a person's wealth.

MONEY TERMS

MONEY, from Latin. Roman money was coined in the temple of Juno Moneta. Our word "mint" can be traced back to the same source.

SALARY, from Latin *salarium*, "salt money," a part of the wages paid to Roman soldiers.

BANK, from Italian *banco*, the bench or counter used by the moneychangers of the Middle Ages.

FEE, from old Teutonic *feoh*, "cattle."

PECUNIARY, from Latin *pecus*, "cattle." Sometimes the word referred to both sheep and cattle.

CAPITAL, from Latin *caput*, "head"— as in "head of cattle."

CHATTEL, from either Latin *caput*, or *catel*, Anglo-Saxon for "wealth."

BRITISH MONEY

POUND, from Latin *pondo*, "weight." The symbol for the pound comes from *libra*, a Roman weight or "pound."

PENNY, from either Dutch *pand*, "pawn," "pledge," or "small token," or Latin *pendo*, "to weigh."

FARTHING, from Old Saxon word for "four." A farthing is a "fourthling."

GUINEA, minted from Guinea gold.

SHILLING, perhaps from German *skil*, "to divide."

FLORIN, from either the Latin name for the city of Florence, or from Italian *florino*, "flower."

CROWN, named originally from the picture of a crown on it.

SOVEREIGN, from picture of the reigning British monarch it bears.

SOME CURRENCY VALUES			
	U.S. $1.00	$2.00	$3.00
Australian pound			
Canadian dollar			
Guatemalan quetzal			
Danish krone			
English pound			
Israeli pound			
Netherlands guilder			

SYMBOLS AND ABBREVIATIONS	
$\frac{1}{4}$d.	farthing
$\frac{1}{2}$d.	halfpenny ("ha'penny")
1d.	penny
3d.	threepenny piece ("thruppence")
6d.	sixpence
1/- or 1s.	shilling ("bob")
2/- or 2s.	florin
2/6 or 2s.6d.	half-a-crown
£	pound

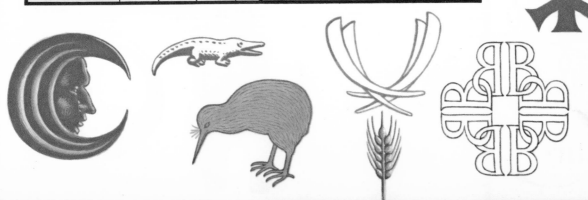

WAYS OF KEEPING COUNT

COUNTING ON FINGERS

Fingers were probably the first counters. The word "digit" now means both "finger" and "numeral."

COUNTING WITH PEBBLES

Our word "calculate" comes from "calculus," the Latin word for "pebble."

COUNTING WITH STICKS

The ancient Chinese used short sticks as counters.

COUNTING BY MAKING NOTCHES IN A STICK

Making notches in a stick was an easy way of counting days as they passed.

COUNTING BY TYING KNOTS IN A CORD

The Incas tied knots in cords in counting the sheaves of grain they reaped.

COUNTING BY MAKING MARKS

We still use this way of keeping tally.

WAYS OF CALCULATING

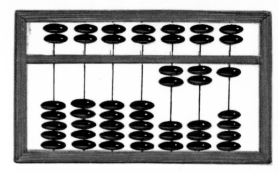

CHINESE ABACUS

With an abacus a person works out a problem by moving beads on wires. Each bead has a value. On the first wire at the right, each bead below the crossbar stands for 1, each bead above for 5. The beads on the second wire stand for 10's below and 50's above, on the third wire for 100's and 500's, and so on.

$$\begin{array}{r} .89 \\ .25 \\ 1.07 \\ \hline 2.21 \end{array}$$

NUMERALS

Calculating with numerals is now, in a great many parts of the world, much more common than calculating with an abacus. Five hundred years ago calculating with numerals was often called "calculating with the pen" to contrast it with calculating with beads or some other counters.

CALCULATING MACHINES

Today there are calculating machines that can add, subtract, multiply, and divide very, very rapidly. Some are rather simple; others are very complicated. A big electronic computer can solve in a few hours a problem that would take a person working with pencil and paper several hundred years to solve.

NUMERALS

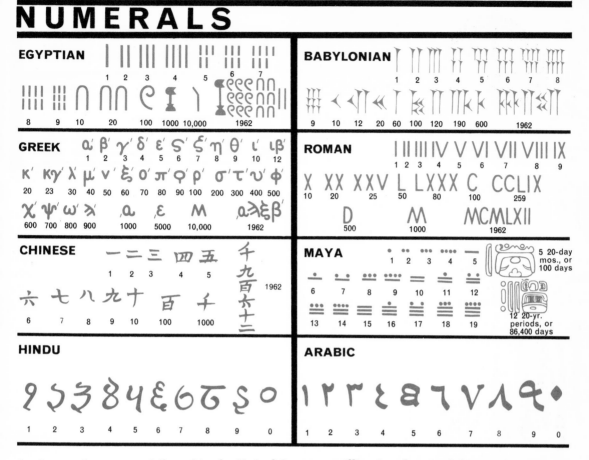

EGYPTIAN — 1 2 3 4 5 6 7, 8 9 10 20 100 1000 10,000 1962

BABYLONIAN — 1 2 3 4 5 6 7 8, 9 10 12 20 60 100 120 190 600 1962

GREEK — α′ β′ γ′ δ′ ε′ ς′ ξ′ η′ θ′ ι′ ιβ′ : 1 2 3 4 5 6 7 8 9 10 12; κ′ κγ′ λ′ μ′ ν′ ξ′ ο′ π′ ϟ′ ρ′ σ′ τ′ υ′ φ′ : 20 23 30 40 50 60 70 80 90 100 200 300 400 500; χ′ ψ′ ω′ ϡ′ ,α ,ε Μ ,αϡξβ′ : 600 700 800 900 1000 5000 10,000 1962

ROMAN — I II III IV V VI VII VIII IX : 1 2 3 4 5 6 7 8 9; X XX XXV L LXXX C CCLIX : 10 20 25 50 80 100 259; D 500 M 1000 MCMLXII 1962

CHINESE — 一 二 三 四 五 : 1 2 3 4 5; 六 七 八 九 十 百 千 : 6 7 8 9 10 100 1000; 千九百六十二 1962

MAYA — 1 2 3 4 5 / 6 7 8 9 10 11 12 / 13 14 15 16 17 18 19; 5 20-day mos., or 100 days; 12 20-yr. periods, or 86,400 days

HINDU — 1 2 3 4 5 6 7 8 9 0

ARABIC — ١ ٢ ٣ ٤ ٥ ٦ ٧ ٨ ٩ ٠ : 1 2 3 4 5 6 7 8 9 0

In the number system followed in the United States, a million is a thousand thousands, a billion a thousand millions, and so on as follows, each a thousand times the one before:

Trillion	Nonillion	Quindecillion
Quadrillion	Decillion	Sexdecillion
Quintillion	Undecillion	Septendecillion
Sextillion	Duodecillion	Octodecillion
Septillion	Tredecillion	Novemdecillion
Octillion	Quattuordecillion	Vigintillion, or

1,000,000,000,000,000,000,000,000,000,000,000,000,000,000,000,000,000,000,000,000,000,000,000

THE ANCIENT EGYPTIAN WAY OF MULTIPLYING AND DIVIDING

The ancient Egyptians added and subtracted just as we do, using their own numerals, of course, but they multiplied and divided by a process of doubling. Let us suppose they wished to multiply 40 by 13. They doubled and redoubled the multiplicand thus:

1 -	40
2 -	80
4 -	160
8 -	320

There would be no point to doubling another time, for the number in the first column would then be 16, which is greater than the multiplier. They then picked out the numbers in the first column which added up to 13 and added the corresponding numbers in the second column to get the product:

1 -	40
4 -	160
8 -	320
13 -	520

These are the steps in dividing 520 by 13:

1 -	13
2 -	26
4 -	52
*8 -	104*
16 -	208
*32 -	416*
40 -	520

MEASURES OF LENGTH

CUBIT

The people of long ago used parts of their own bodies in measuring. The cubit was the length of the forearm. The cubit is often mentioned in the Bible.

DIGIT The digit was the width of a finger.

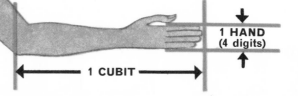

HAND

The hand was the width of the hand, or palm. It is now four inches and is used in measuring the height of horses.

FOOT

The foot was the length of the foot.

SPAN

The span was the distance from the end of the thumb to the end of the little finger with the hand spread out.

TABLES OF LENGTH

MEASURES OF LENGTH (English system)

12 inches	= 1 foot
3 feet	= 1 yard
5½ yards (16½ feet)	= 1 rod
40 rods	= 1 furlong
8 furlongs (1760 yards or 5280 feet)	= 1 mile

MEASURES OF LENGTH (metric system)

10 millimeters	= 1 centimeter
10 centimeters	= 1 decimeter
10 decimeters (100 centimeters or 1000 millimeters)	= 1 meter
1000 meters	= 1 kilometer

Comparisons:

1 inch	= 2.54 centimeters
1 foot	= 0.3048 meters
1 yard	= 0.9144 meters
1 mile	= 1.6093 kilometers
1 centimeter	= 0.3937 inches
1 meter	= 3.2808 feet
1 kilometer	= 0.62137 miles

NAUTICAL MEASURE (English system)

6 feet	= 1 fathom
100 fathoms	= 1 cable's length
10 cable lengths	= 1 nautical mile

Comparisons:

1 nautical mile	= 1.15157 miles
1 nautical mile	= 1853.2 meters

YARD

Henry I of England in the 12th century decreed that the yard was to be the distance from the end of his nose to the end of his thumb.

FURLONG

"Furlong" is short for "furrow long." A farmer could plow a furrow just so long before he needed to let his oxen rest a while.

INCH

In the beginning the inch was the width of the thumb. In the 14th century Edward II of England decreed that an inch was to be three barleycorns (grains of barley) laid end to end.

1 YARD

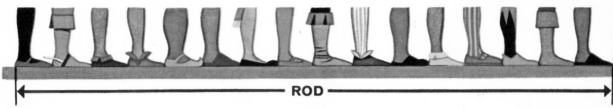

ROD

ROD

In the 16th century the length of the rod was set by having sixteen men as they were coming out of church put their left feet one behind the other.

MILE

The word "mile" is short for *mille passuum*, the Latin words for "1,000 paces."

PACE   A pace was a double step.

MEASURES OF AREA

ACRE

Four furrows, a furlong long and an oxgoad apart, was the measure of the first acre.

TABLES OF AREA

MEASURES OF AREA (English system)

144 square inches	= 1 square foot
9 square feet	= 1 square yard
30¼ square yards	= 1 square rod
160 square rods	= 1 acre
640 acres	= 1 square mile

MEASURES OF AREA (metric system)

100 square millimeters	= 1 square centimeter
100 square centimeters	= 1 square decimeter
100 square decimeters	= 1 square meter
100 square meters	= 1 are
100 ares	= 1 hectare
100 hectares	= 1 square kilometer

Comparisons:

1 acre	= 40.4687 ares
1 square mile	= 259 hectares
1 hectare	= 2.471 acres
1 square kilometer	= 0.3861 square miles

MEASURES OF WEIGHT

STONE

The Babylonians used polished stones as weights. They used different stones for weighing different things. Today in England a "stone" is 14 pounds.

SHEKEL

The Babylonians, Hebrews, and other people of the Near East had coins called shekels. The name came from the name of a Babylonian unit of weight.

CARAT

The Arabs used the seeds of the carob tree as weights. The "carat" now used in weighing diamonds began as a "carob seed."

GRAIN

One grain of wheat is very much like another. The ancient Greeks and Egyptians used grains of wheat as weights. The "grain" of today thus had its beginning long ago.

POUND

The story of the pound begins with the Greeks. The word comes from a word for "weight." The abbreviation (lb.) comes from *libra*, the Latin word for pound.

OUNCE

The Romans divided their pound into 12 *unciae*. The *uncia* became our ounce, but we have 16 ounces in a pound when we weigh common materials.

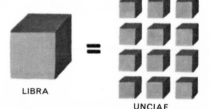

LIBRA

UNCIAE

ENGLISH SYSTEM		
Troy Weight (Jewels, precious metals)	**Avoirdupois Weight** (Ordinary commodities)	**Apothecaries' Weight** (Drugs)
3.086 grains = 1 carat	16 drams = 1 ounce	20 grains = 1 scruple
24 grains = 1 pennyweight	16 ounces = 1 pound	3 scruples = 1 dram
20 pennyweights = 1 ounce	7000 grains = 1 pound	8 drams = 1 ounce
12 ounces = 1 pound	14 pounds = 1 stone	12 ounces = 1 pound
	2000 pounds = 1 ton	
	2240 pounds = 1 long ton	

METRIC SYSTEM	COMPARISONS
10 milligrams = 1 centigram	1 ounce (avoirdupois) = 28.3495 grams
100 centigrams = 1 gram	1 pound (avoirdupois) = 453.39 grams
1000 grams = 1 kilogram	1 ton = 907.18 kilograms or .907 metric tons
1000 kilograms = 1 metric ton	1 gram = 15.432 grains
	1 kilogram = 2.2046 pounds (avoirdupois)
	1 metric ton = 2204.6 pounds (avoirdupois)

MEASURES OF CAPACITY

GILL   PINT   QUART   GALLON

GALLON, QUART, PINT, GILL

The name "gallon" is supposed to have come from an old French word for "bowl." "Quart" is short for "quarter gallon." (There came to be a slightly different quart for measuring dry materials.) The name "pint" comes from the *painted* mark on old vessels for measuring. "Gill," strangely, comes from an old word for "tub."

HOGSHEAD

In England in 1423 the hogshead was made a standard measure for measuring liquids. It gets its name from a kind of cask or barrel called a hogshead.

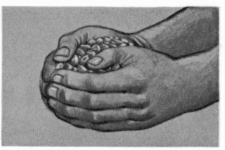

HANDFUL

The American Indians measured corn by the handful. The handful is a common measure of capacity among primitive peoples.

HEAP

The heap has also been a common measure of capacity among primitive peoples. It is, of course, not at all accurate.

GOURDFUL

American Indians measured liquids by the gourdful. It goes without saying that the measure is not accurate, because gourds vary in size.

ENGLISH SYSTEM

Dry Measure	Apothecaries' Fluid Measure	Liquid Measure
2 pints = 1 quart	60 minims = 1 fluid dram	4 gills = 1 pint
8 quarts = 1 peck	8 fluid drams = 1 fluid ounce	2 pints = 1 quart
4 pecks = 1 bushel	16 (U.S.) fluid ounces = 1 pint	4 quarts = 1 gallon
	20 (British) fluid ounces = 1 imperial pint	
	8 pints = 1 gallon (U.S.)	
	8 imperial pints = 1 imperial gallon	

METRIC SYSTEM

10 milliliters = 1 centiliter
10 centiliters = 1 deciliter
10 deciliters = 1 liter
10 liters = 1 decaliter
10 decaliters = 1 hectoliter
10 hectoliters = 1 kiloliter

COMPARISONS

1 bushel = 35.2383 liters
1 dry quart = 1.1012 liters
1 liquid quart = .9463 liters
1 centiliter = .338 fluid ounces
1 liter = .9081 dry quarts or 1.0567 liquid quarts
1 hectoliter = 2.838 bushels or 26.418 gallons

TERMS USED IN ASTRONOMY

APHELION. The earth's orbit is not a perfect circle. The point at which it is farthest from the sun is the aphelion.

APOGEE. The point in its orbit at which the moon is farthest from the earth is the apogee.

ASTEROIDS. Asteroids are very tiny planets. They are sometimes called planetoids. Most asteroids have orbits between the orbits of Mars and Jupiter.

COMET. The word "comet" comes from "coma," the Latin word for "hair." A comet gets its name from the tail of gas and dust that streams out from it when it is within 200 million miles or so of the sun.

CONJUNCTION. When two heavenly bodies are in exactly the same direction from the earth, we say that they are in conjunction.

CONSTELLATION. The word "constellation" means "stars together." Originally a constellation was simply a group of stars which seem to be close together as viewed from the earth. To astronomers now a constellation is, more exactly, a section of the heavens named for the chief group of stars in it. There are 88 constellations.

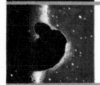

DARK NEBULA. A dark nebula is a vast cloud of star dust and gas not close enough to any stars to be lighted up by them. A famous dark nebula is the Horsehead Nebula.

DAY. A sidereal day is the time it takes a moon or a planet to turn around once on its axis. A solar day is the average time from noon (when the sun is highest in the sky for the day) to noon. The earth's solar day, because of the earth's travels around the sun, is about 4 minutes longer than its sidereal day. Our calendar is based on the solar day. The sidereal days in a year number one more than the solar days.

ECLIPSE. An eclipse occurs when one heavenly body gets wholly or partly into the shadow of another.

GALAXY. A galaxy is a vast group of stars. Our sun is in the galaxy called the Milky Way. A galaxy is sometimes called a star city or an island universe.

METEOR. Meteors are small bodies, many no larger than a grain of sand, which travel around the sun. Every day millions enter the earth's atmosphere. As they fall through the air they become white-hot and are called shooting stars or, if large enough, fireballs.

METEORITE. Most meteors that enter the earth's atmosphere turn to vapor before they reach the earth's surface. Those that do reach the earth's surface are called meteorites.

MOON. A moon is a heavenly body which travels around a planet. The earth has only one moon while Jupiter has twelve.

NEBULA. A nebula is a great cloud of gas and star dust far out in space. A nebula glows like a distant star if it is lighted up by light from stars nearby.

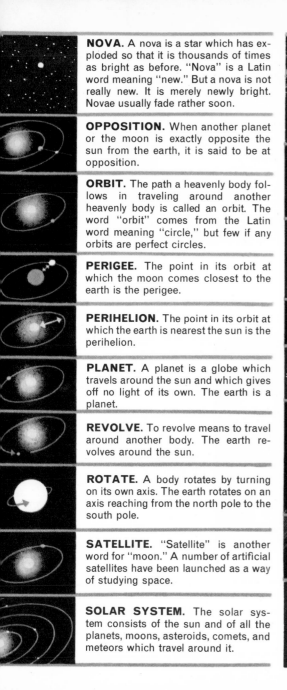

NOVA. A nova is a star which has exploded so that it is thousands of times as bright as before. "Nova" is a Latin word meaning "new." But a nova is not really new. It is merely newly bright. Novae usually fade rather soon.

OPPOSITION. When another planet or the moon is exactly opposite the sun from the earth, it is said to be at opposition.

ORBIT. The path a heavenly body follows in traveling around another heavenly body is called an orbit. The word "orbit" comes from the Latin word meaning "circle," but few if any orbits are perfect circles.

PERIGEE. The point in its orbit at which the moon comes closest to the earth is the perigee.

PERIHELION. The point in its orbit at which the earth is nearest the sun is the perihelion.

PLANET. A planet is a globe which travels around the sun and which gives off no light of its own. The earth is a planet.

REVOLVE. To revolve means to travel around another body. The earth revolves around the sun.

ROTATE. A body rotates by turning on its own axis. The earth rotates on an axis reaching from the north pole to the south pole.

SATELLITE. "Satellite" is another word for "moon." A number of artificial satellites have been launched as a way of studying space.

SOLAR SYSTEM. The solar system consists of the sun and of all the planets, moons, asteroids, comets, and meteors which travel around it.

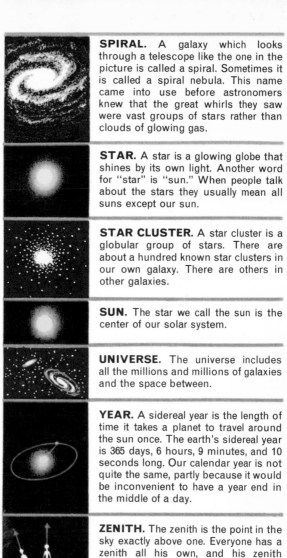

SPIRAL. A galaxy which looks through a telescope like the one in the picture is called a spiral. Sometimes it is called a spiral nebula. This name came into use before astronomers knew that the great whirls they saw were vast groups of stars rather than clouds of glowing gas.

STAR. A star is a glowing globe that shines by its own light. Another word for "star" is "sun." When people talk about the stars they usually mean all suns except our sun.

STAR CLUSTER. A star cluster is a globular group of stars. There are about a hundred known star clusters in our own galaxy. There are others in other galaxies.

SUN. The star we call the sun is the center of our solar system.

UNIVERSE. The universe includes all the millions and millions of galaxies and the space between.

YEAR. A sidereal year is the length of time it takes a planet to travel around the sun once. The earth's sidereal year is 365 days, 6 hours, 9 minutes, and 10 seconds long. Our calendar year is not quite the same, partly because it would be inconvenient to have a year end in the middle of a day.

ZENITH. The zenith is the point in the sky exactly above one. Everyone has a zenith all his own, and his zenith changes as he moves about.

ZODIAC. The zodiac is made up of the constellations along the path which the sun appears to follow in the course of a year. Because of the journey of the earth around the sun, the sun appears to be in first one constellation and then another.

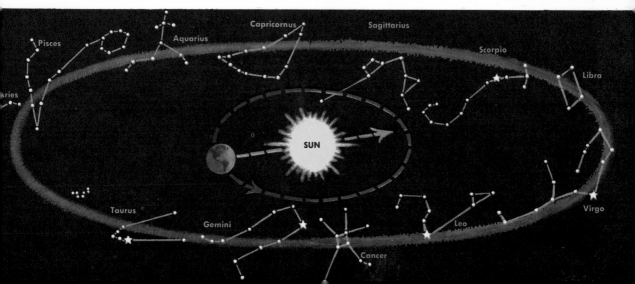

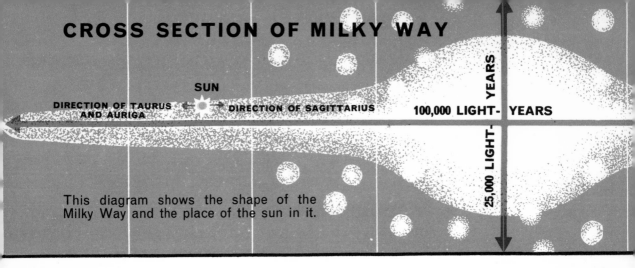

CROSS SECTION OF MILKY WAY

SUN

DIRECTION OF TAURUS AND AURIGA ← ○ → DIRECTION OF SAGITTARIUS

100,000 LIGHT-YEARS

100,000 LIGHT-YEARS

25,000 LIGHT-YEARS

This diagram shows the shape of the Milky Way and the place of the sun in it.

ASTRONOMICAL NUMBERS

As the earth whirls on its axis, a spot on the equator moves a little more than 1,000 miles an hour.

The earth travels about 1,100 miles a minute (18½ miles a second) in its journey around the sun. In a day it travels more than 1½ million miles.

Strangely enough, the diameter of the earth's orbit is almost exactly 1,000 times the distance light travels in one second.

The earth's yearly journey around the sun is nearly 600 million miles. Every ten-year-old has traveled nearly six billion miles even if he has never been away from home.

The sun and its planets move about 170 miles a second as the Milky Way galaxy whirls around. Even so it takes the sun some 200 million years to make one swing around the center of the galaxy.

The galaxies in the universe are rushing away from one another. Some are traveling as fast as 70,000 miles a second.

It would take more than one million earths to make a ball as large as the sun.

Some of the great "flames" that shoot up from the sun (solar prominences) are hundreds of thousands of miles high. The record height is 1,050,000 miles.

It would take 27 billion suns to make a ball as large as the giant red star Epsilon Aurigae.

About one million meteors reach our atmosphere every hour. All but a very, very, very few turn to vapor before they reach the earth's surface. But in space travel meteors would be a real danger.

There are at least 100 billion stars in our Milky Way galaxy.

Galaxies are not all shaped like our Milky Way. But all galaxies are great "star cities" made up of vast numbers of stars. Sometimes they are called "island universes."

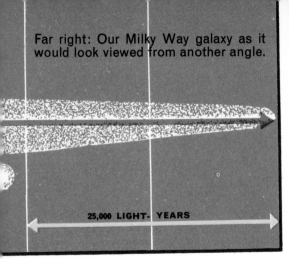

Far right: Our Milky Way galaxy as it would look viewed from another angle.

25,000 LIGHT- YEARS

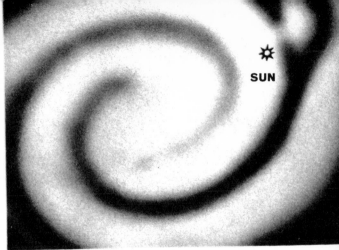

SUN

There are known to be more than a billion galaxies in the universe. There may be several billions.

If all the stars in the Milky Way galaxy had names, it would take 4,000 years to say all their names if they could be said one every second without stopping.

In all the galaxies together there are probably as many stars as there are grains of sand on all the world's seashores.

Our sun's nearest star neighbor is about 25 trillion miles away.

In spite of all the billions and billions of stars, space is not crowded. It is no more crowded with stars than North America would be with chipmunks if there were only three of them scampering about over the entire continent.

The distance across our Milky Way galaxy is about 100,000 light-years (100,000 times 6 trillion miles).

Our sun is about 30,000 light-years (30,000 times 6 trillion miles) from the center of the Milky Way galaxy.

The Great Spiral in Andromeda is the nearest galaxy shaped like our Milky Way. It is more than 2 million light-years away (2 million times 6 trillion miles).

The farthest galaxies our telescopes show are 2 billion light-years away.

The temperature on the surface of the sun is 11,000° F. In the interior it is 30 million degrees.

In a year the sun uses up 22 quadrillion tons of its hydrogen in producing the energy it gives off. But even so it has enough to last for billions of years to come. It has about one octillion, 494 septillion tons.

The Crab Nebula is a great cloud of gas that stretches for 17,700 billion miles. For more than 5,000 years it has been spreading out at the rate of 684 miles a second.

A tablespoonful of the material from a white dwarf star would weigh a ton or more if it could be brought to the earth.

Gravity on the surface of the white dwarf companion of Sirius is 250,000 times as great as gravity on the earth's surface.

STAR MAGNITUDES

LEO

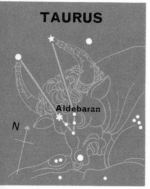

TAURUS

Aldebaran

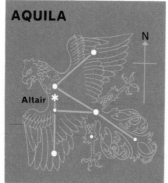

AQUILA

N

Altair

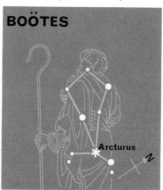

BOÖTES

Arcturus

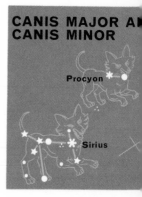

CANIS MAJOR A
CANIS MINOR

Procyon

Sirius

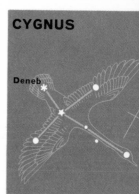

LYRA

Vega

N

CYGNUS

Deneb

Stars are grouped into magnitudes according to their brightness as seen from the earth. How bright a star looks in a moonless, cloudless night sky depends on how much light it gives off and how far away it is.

First-magnitude stars are, on the average, 2½ times as bright as second-magnitude stars; second-magnitude stars are 2½ times as bright as third-magnitude stars; and so on. First-magnitude stars are about 100 times as bright as sixth-magnitude stars. Without binoculars or a telescope, no one can see stars fainter than magnitude 6.

The magnitudes of the very brightest few stars are —1 or 0.

On star maps different symbols are used for stars of different magnitudes. These are the symbols used in these constellation maps.

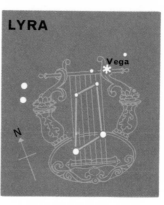

1

✳ 1st magnitude or brighter   ● 3rd magnitude

★ 2nd magnitude   • 4th or 5th magnitude

ORION

Betelgeuse

Rigel

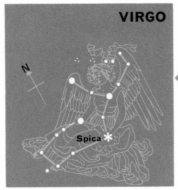

VIRGO

N

Spica

CONSTELLATIONS CONTAINING FOURTEEN OF THE TWENTY-ONE BRIGHTEST STARS

(Notice that Auriga contains the bright star Capella and that Orion has two bright stars.)

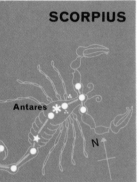

SCORPIUS

Antares

N

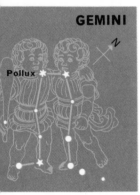

GEMINI

Pollux

THE TWENTY-ONE BRIGHTEST STARS IN THE ORDER OF THEIR BRIGHTNESS

STAR	DISTANCE IN LIGHT-YEARS	CONSTELLATION
Sirius	9	Canis Major (The Great Dog)
Canopus	98	Carina (The Keel of the Ship)
Alpha Centauri	4	Centaurus (The Centaur)
Arcturus	36	Boötes (The Herdsman)
Vega	26	Lyra (The Lyre)
Capella	45	Auriga (The Charioteer)
Rigel	900	Orion (The Hunter)
Procyon	11	Canis Minor (The Little Dog)
Achernar	118	Eridanus (The River)
Beta Centauri	490	Centaurus (The Centaur)
Betelgeuse	600	Orion (The Hunter)
Altair	16	Aquila (The Eagle)
Aldebaran	68	Taurus (The Bull)
Alpha Crucis	370	Crux (The Southern Cross)
Antares	520	Scorpius (The Scorpion)
Spica	220	Virgo (The Virgin)
Fomalhaut	23	Piscis Austrinus (The Southern Fish)
Pollux	35	Gemini (The Twins)
Deneb	1600	Cygnus (The Swan)
Beta Crucis	490	Crux (The Southern Cross)
Regulus	84	Leo (The Lion)

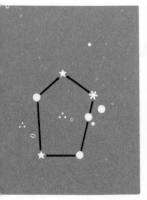

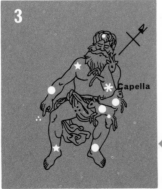

Capella

AURIGA

1. The stars of Auriga
2. Auriga as it is usually shown on a star map
3. The picture Auriga made to people of long ago–a chariot eer with young goats

SKY DISTANCES

EARTH ●————— Astronomical Unit —————▶ SUN

Units of Measurement Used by Astronomers

ASTRONOMICAL UNIT:
Average distance from the earth to the sun (roughly 93,000,000 miles)

LIGHT-YEAR:
Distance light travels in one year (roughly 6,000,000,000,000 miles, since light travels at the rate of 186,272 miles per second)

PARSEC:
3.26 light-years (roughly 19,000,000,000,000 miles)

The little scenes suggest what was happening on the earth when the light that reaches our eyes tonight left these heavenly bodies. It takes light from the sun only eight minutes to reach us.

ALPHA CENTAURI

ARCTURUS

4.3 LIGHT-YEARS

36 LIGHT-YEARS

34,000 LIGHT-YEARS

120,000,000 LIGHT-YEARS

4,100 LIGHT-YEARS

1,000 LIGHT-YEARS

2,300,000 LIGHT-YEARS

68 LIGHT-YEARS

220 LIGHT-YEARS

600 LIGHT-YEARS

900 LIGHT-YEARS

ALDEBARAN

SPICA

BETELGEUSE

Colonial Times in America

Aztec Calendar Stone

Earliest Automobiles

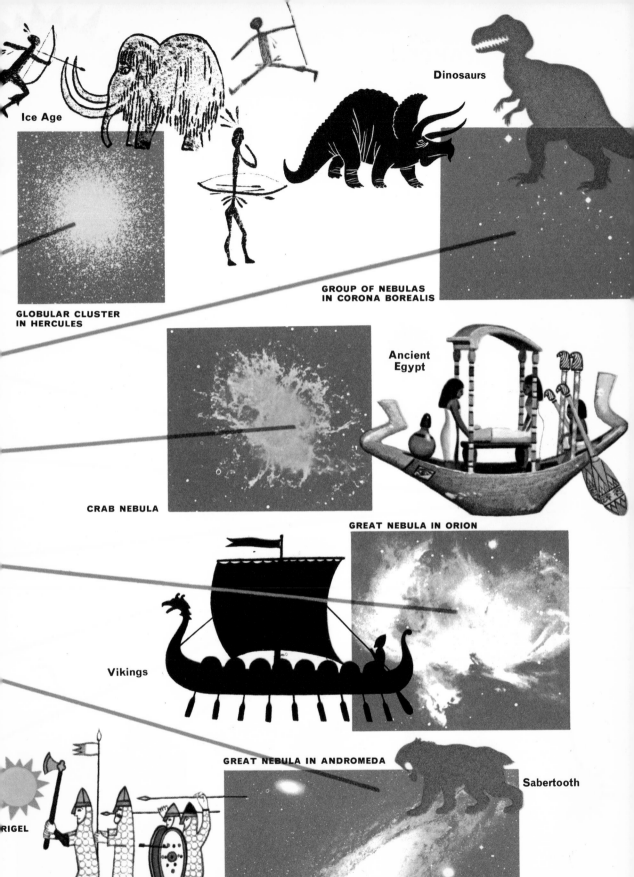

Ice Age

Dinosaurs

GLOBULAR CLUSTER
IN HERCULES

GROUP OF NEBULAS
IN CORONA BOREALIS

CRAB NEBULA

Ancient
Egypt

GREAT NEBULA IN ORION

Vikings

GREAT NEBULA IN ANDROMEDA

Sabertooth

RIGEL

Norman Conquest

THE SUN

MERCURY •

VENUS •

EARTH •

MARS •

JUPITER

SATURN

URANUS

NEPTUNE

PLUTO •

The sun is a yellow star. The sun is 865,000 miles in diameter; if it were hollow, there would be room inside it for 1,300,000 earths. It is 700 times as large as all its planets, moons, asteroids, comets, and meteors put together.

The sun weighs 330,000 times as much as the earth.

A boy who weighed 100 pounds on the earth would weigh nearly 1½ tons at the surface of the sun.

The temperature at the center of the sun is about 30,000,000° F. The temperature at the surface is about 11,000° F. Strangely enough, the temperature in the corona is about 1,000,000° F.

The tongues of glowing gas called prominences often shoot up more than 100,000 miles from the surface.

Sunspots are great storms on the surface of the sun. A big sunspot could swallow up dozens of earths.

The temperature in a sunspot is some 3,000 degrees lower than at other places on the sun's surface, but it is far from low.

Sunspots come in eleven-year cycles: for 5 or 6 years the number gradually increases and then for 5 or 6 years it diminishes. There have been periods when for many years there have been very few. One such period was between 1798 and 1833.

The sun rotates on its axis, but some parts rotate faster than others. The period of rotation is about 25 days at the equator, and about 33 days at the poles. Such a difference is possible because the sun is not solid.

A great many of the chemical elements found here on earth are known to exist in the sun, but 95% of the sun's material consists of hydrogen and helium.

Energy is produced in the sun much as it is produced in a hydrogen bomb: hydrogen is changed to helium.

One day from the time you read this sentence the sun will be about 345 billion tons lighter. For every second 564 million tons of hydrogen is changed into only 560 million tons of helium. The sun therefore loses roughly 4 million tons a second.

Although its hydrogen is being used up at a terrific rate, the sun has enough left—some 1 octillion, 494 septillion tons—to last for billions of years.

The earth gets less than $\frac{1}{2,000,000,000}$ of the energy the sun sends out. If the people of the United States had to pay for the energy they get from the sun at the same rate they pay for electricity from power plants, the yearly bill would be more than 300 million billion dollars.

If the sun sputtered out and no longer gave us light and heat, all the earth's stores of coal, petroleum, and other fuels could keep the earth as warm as it is now for only three days.

Solar batteries can now convert the energy of the sun's rays directly into a usable electric current.

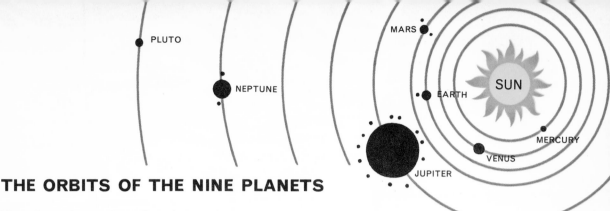

THE ORBITS OF THE NINE PLANETS

This chart shows the order of the orbits of the nine planets in
our solar system. It does not show the comparative distances of
these orbits from the sun. In a book the planets and their orbits
cannot be drawn to the same scale if the planets are made large
enough to be seen. Actually, most of the solar system is empty
space. If, in making a model of the solar system, a beach ball
thirty inches across was used for the sun, a radish seed would be
about the right size for Pluto. And, if the same scale used in
choosing the models were used in placing them, the radish seed
for Pluto would have to be put nearly two miles from the beach-
ball representing the sun!

PLANET STATISTICS

Planet	Symbol	Average Distance from the Sun in Millions of Miles	Diameter in Miles	Length of Time Taken for Revolution around Sun	Length of Time Taken for Rotation on Axis	Number of Known Moons
Mercury	☿	36	3,000	88 days	88 days	0
Venus	♀	67	7,600	225 days	225 days (?)	0
Earth	⊕	93	7,900	365 ¼ days	23 hr. 56 min.	1
Mars	♂	142	4,200	687 days	24 hr. 37 min.	2
Jupiter	♃	483	87,000	12 years	9 hr. 50 min.	12
Saturn	♄	886	71,500	29 ½ years	10 hr. 2 min.	9
Uranus	♅	1,783	29,500	84 years	10 hr. 48 min.	5
Neptune	♆	2,791	26,800	165 years	15 hr. 48 min.	2
Pluto	♇	3,671	3,600	248 years	6 ½ days (?)	0
Sun	☉		864,000		25 days	

BRIGHTNESS OF THE PLANETS

The planets all vary in brightness because, as
a result of their travels around the sun, they
are at varying distances from the earth.
MERCURY at its brightest is brighter than
Sirius, the Dog Star, the brightest true star.
It is, however, almost always hidden by the
glare of the sun.
VENUS is the brightest of all the planets—
much brighter than the Dog Star. Venus is so
bright that it can sometimes be seen in the
daytime.
MARS at its brightest is brighter than Mercury
but not so bright as Venus. It looks like a
reddish star.

JUPITER always looks like a bright yellowish
star. At their brightest Jupiter and Mars are
about equally bright. At their palest Jupiter
is much brighter than Mars.
SATURN at its brightest is brighter than all the
true stars except Sirius and Canopus. It is
not, however, nearly so bright as Mars, Jupiter, Mercury, and Venus at their brightest.
URANUS is not bright enough to be seen with
the naked eye by most people.
NEPTUNE can be seen only with a powerful
telescope.
PLUTO is very faint and very, very hard to
locate even with a 12-inch telescope.

COULD PEOPLE LIVE ON ANY OF THE OTHER PLANETS IN OUR SOLAR SYSTEM?

To be a possible home for people, a planet must have a fairly mild temperature, at least in some areas; a solid surface, at least in part; an atmosphere containing oxygen, but no poisonous gases; water; green plants to furnish food; and sunlight. The chart below shows whether, so far as scientists now know, any of the other planets in the solar system meet these requirements.

	MERCURY	VENUS	MARS
TEMPERATURE	One half always very hot (about 650° F.); the other half always extremely cold (about —450° F.).	Hot. Surface protected somewhat by thick clouds. Surface temperature probably reaches 250° F.	Great extremes. In summer temperatur may reach more tha 100° F. in daytime a fall to far below zere at night. Winters ve cold.
WATER	No evidence	Probably some, but amount not known. Heavy clouds may be formed of dust or oil droplets, not water.	Some, but not a gre amount.
ATMOSPHERE	Little, if any, atmosphere.	Dense atmosphere, containing a great deal of carbon dioxide. No evidence of oxygen.	Very thin atmosphe made up mostly of nitrogen and argon. Small amounts of ca bon dioxide and prc ably of oxygen prese
GREEN PLANTS	No evidence.	Not determined because of dense clouds covering surface.	Some very simple li ing things thought be present. Perhaps plants somewhat lik lichens.
SOLID SURFACE	Yes	Bare possibility that its rocky surface is covered with a deep ocean of water or oil.	Yes
SUNLIGHT	Intense sunlight on one side; none on the other.	Yes, but very little can shine through the heavy clouds to the planet's surface.	Yes
ANSWER	NO	**?**	NO

JUPITER	SATURN	URANUS	NEPTUNE	PLUTO
emely cold. Aver- temperature about 0° F.	Extremely cold. Aver- age temperature about —225° F.	Extremely cold. Average temperature about —300° F.	Extremely cold. Average temperature about —325° F.	Extremely cold. Average temperature about —350° F.
en, if any is ent.	Rings made partly of ice crystals.	No evidence.	No evidence.	No evidence.
se atmosphere e up chiefly of ogen, marsh gas, ammonia, all poi- us or suffocating.	Atmosphere much like Jupiter's.	Not known.	Not known.	Not known.
	No	No	No	No
ace perhaps liq- Planet may, how- be surrounded by ell of ice.	Probably only inner- most core solid. May, however, be sur- rounded by a thick shell of ice.	Not known.	Not known.	Not known.
but too weak to much heating t.	Yes, but too weak to have much heating effect.	Yes, but very weak.	Yes, but very weak.	Yes, but much more like our moonlight than our sunlight.
	NO	NO	NO	NO

TIDES

High tides occur on opposite sides of the earth at the same time. The moon pulls up the water on the part of the earth nearest it. On the opposite side of the earth, where the pull is least, the water bulges away from the moon.

High tides are much higher along certain coasts than along others. The highest tides known occur in the Bay of Fundy, between Nova Scotia and New Brunswick. Sometimes the high tide is 70 feet higher than the low tide there.

High tides come at different times each day because of the traveling of the moon around the earth.

High tides are on the average 12 hours and 25 minutes apart.

The sun also causes tides, but the moon is so much closer to the earth that the tides it causes are much more noticeable. But when the sun, earth, and moon are in a straight line —at new moon and full moon—the sun and moon are causing tides in the same place at the same time and the tides are higher than usual. These extra-high tides are called spring tides. When the moon is at first quarter or last quarter, the sun and moon are pulling at right angles to each other and we have tides less high than usual—neap tides.

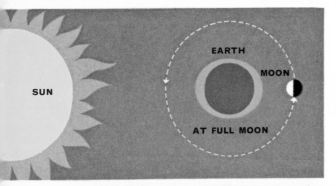

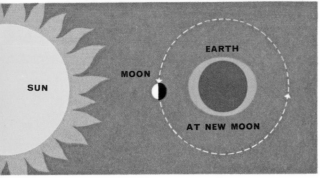

LUNAR ECLIPSES

An eclipse of the moon is called a lunar eclipse.

There cannot be an eclipse of the moon unless the moon is full.

A lunar eclipse can be seen everywhere on the side of the earth toward the moon.

When the moon is wholly in the earth's shadow, the eclipse is called total.

Even when the moon is wholly in the earth's shadow, it does not disappear. It looks dull red because the earth's atmosphere bends some red rays so that they strike it.

In any one spot, a total eclipse lasts for about 2 hours.

A partial eclipse occurs when the moon passes through the edge of the earth's shadow.

There are never more than three lunar eclipses in a year, and there may be none.

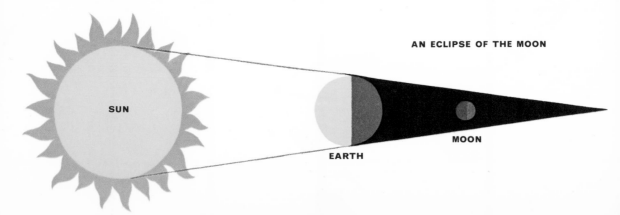

AN ECLIPSE OF THE MOON

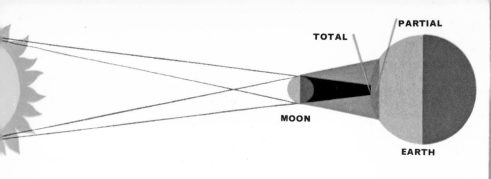

TOTAL
PARTIAL
MOON
EARTH

TOTAL ECLIPSE

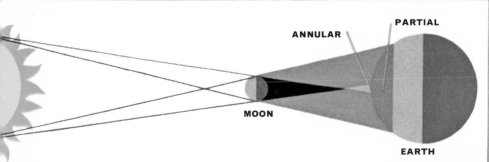

ANNULAR
PARTIAL
MOON
EARTH

ANNULAR ECLIPSE

SOLAR ECLIPSES

An eclipse of the sun is called a solar eclipse.

There cannot be an eclipse of the sun except at the time of the new moon.

If the view of the whole disk of the sun is shut off by the moon, we say that the eclipse is total. If the view of all the disk except a narrow rim around the edge is shut off, we say that the eclipse is annular. All other eclipses are partial.

Of all solar eclipses only about 28 per cent are total.

At the time of a total eclipse the beautiful corona of the sun comes into view.

When the moon hides the sun from part of the earth, that part of the earth is really in the moon's shadow. The path of an eclipse is the path of the moon's shadow.

There are always at least two solar eclipses in a year, and there may be five.

In one place a total solar eclipse never lasts more than eight minutes. Its path is only about 100 miles wide.

MAP SHOWING THE PATHS OF COMING TOTAL ECLIPSES OF THE SUN

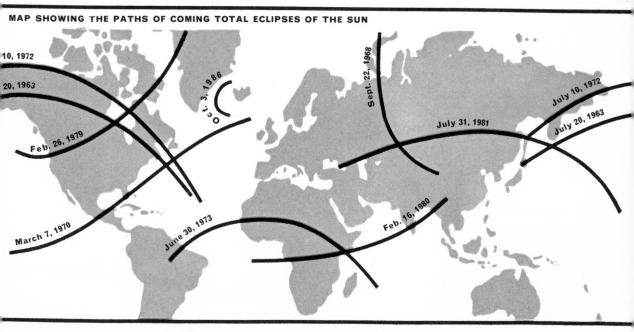

10, 1972

20, 1963

Oct. 31, 1986

Feb. 26, 1979

March 7, 1970

June 30, 1973

Sept. 22, 1968

July 31, 1981

Feb. 16, 1980

July 10, 1972

July 20, 1963

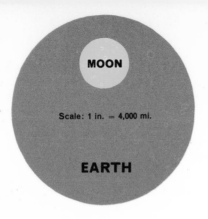

Scale: 1 in. = 4,000 mi.

MOON

EARTH

HOW THE EARTH AND ITS MOON COMPARE IN SIZE

GANYMEDE
(Jupiter III)

CALLISTO
(Jupiter IV)

Scale: 1 in. = 45,000 mi.

JUPITER

HOW JUPITER AND ITS LARGEST MOONS COMPARE IN SIZE

MOONS

PLANET	SATELLITE	YEAR OF DISCOVERY	ESTIMATED DIAMETER IN MILES
EARTH	Moon		2160
MARS	Deimos	1877	5
	Phobos	1877	10
JUPITER	Io (I)	1610	2300
	Europa (II)	1610	2000
	Ganymede (III)	1610	3200
	Callisto (IV)	1610	3200
	Amalthea (V)	1892	120
	VI	1904	100
	VII	1905	40
	VIII	1908	40
	IX	1914	20
	X	1938	15
	XI	1938	20
	XII	1951	15
SATURN	Titan	1655	2600
	Iapetus	1671	1000
	Rhea	1672	1100
	Dione	1684	700
	Tethys	1684	800
	Mimas	1789	400
	Enceladus	1789	500
	Hyperion	1848	300
	Phoebe	1898	200
URANUS	Titania	1787	1000
	Oberon	1787	900
	Ariel	1851	600
	Umbriel	1851	400
	Miranda	1948	150
NEPTUNE	Triton	1846	3000
	Nereid	1949	200

SATELLITES

The earth has one satellite, or moon. Five of the other planets have moons. Some of their moons are larger than the earth's moon, but none is as big as the earth's moon in proportion to the planet it travels around. As the table above shows, most of the moons in the solar system are a great deal smaller than the earth's moon.

How big a moon would look from the surface of the planet it travels around depends not only on the moon's size but also on how far away it is from the planet. Phobos, the larger of the two moons of Mars, would look about a third as big as our moon even though our moon is more than 200 times as big. Phobos is only 3,700 miles from the surface of Mars while our moon is, on the average, 239,000 miles from the surface of the earth. Jupiter's largest moons are more than 650,000 miles from the surface of Jupiter.

Moons differ greatly in the length of time it takes them to circle their planets. Phobos needs only 7 hours and 39 minutes to circle Mars, while Jupiter IX needs 758 days for its journey around Jupiter. The moon circles the earth in about 27⅓ days.

HOW THE LARGER MOONS
IN THE SOLAR SYSTEM COMPARE IN SIZE
WITH THE PLANET MERCURY
SCALE: 1 IN. = 1,500 MI.

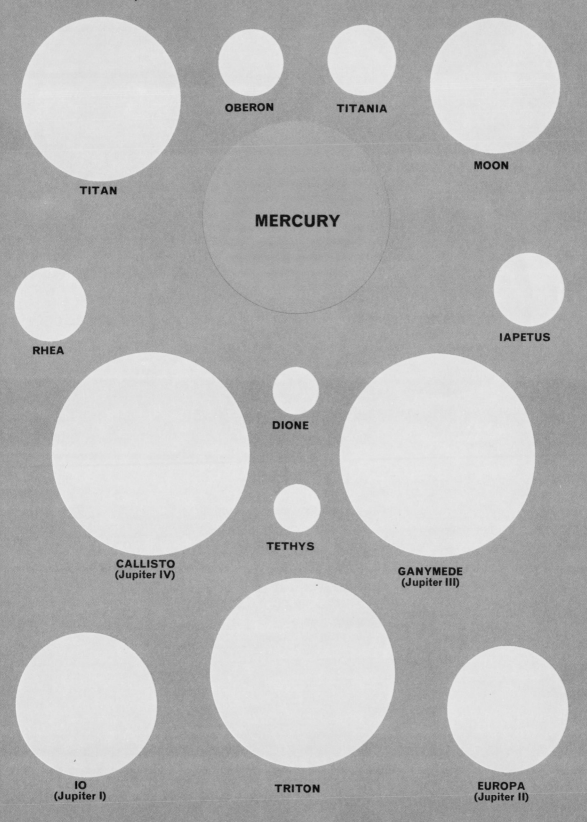

TITAN

OBERON

TITANIA

MOON

MERCURY

RHEA

IAPETUS

DIONE

CALLISTO
(Jupiter IV)

TETHYS

GANYMEDE
(Jupiter III)

IO
(Jupiter I)

TRITON

EUROPA
(Jupiter II)

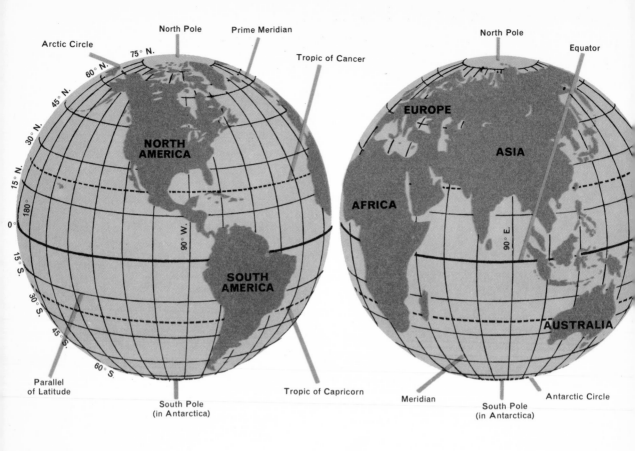

EARTH FIGURES

Diameter of earth at equator: 7,926.68 miles.
Circumference of earth at equator: 24,902.39 miles.
Diameter of earth from pole to pole: 7,900.00 miles.
Circumference of earth through poles: 24,860.49 miles.
Length of a degree of latitude at the equator: 68.704 miles.
> (The length of a degree of latitude would be the same everywhere if the earth were a perfect sphere. The slight flattening at the poles makes the length of a degree of latitude slightly greater in the polar regions.)

Length of a degree of longitude at the equator: 69.17 miles.
> (The length of a degree of longitude is greatest at the equator. It decreases gradually toward the poles.)

Area of earth's surface: 196,950,284 square miles.
Volume of earth: About 259,000,000,000 cubic miles.
Weight of earth: 6,588,000,000,000,000,000,000 tons.
Time needed for one rotation on axis: 23 hours, 56 minutes, 4.09 seconds.
> (This period of time is called the sidereal [star] day. The day we use in our calendar-making is the solar [sun] day, which averages 24 hours.)

Time needed for one journey around the sun: 365 days, 6 hours, 9 minutes, 9.5 seconds.
Speed of a point on the equator as the earth rotates: About $17\frac{1}{2}$ miles per minute.
Average speed at which the earth travels around the sun: $18\frac{1}{2}$ miles per second.
Speed at which the sun is carrying the earth around the center of the Milky Way galaxy: 170 miles per second.
Speed at which the galaxy is drifting through space: More than 170 miles per second.

GLOBAL FACTS

No one can ever see the sun straight overhead if he is north of the Tropic of Cancer or south of the Tropic of Capricorn.

"Due east toward the rising sun" is a well-known expression, but actually the sun, except at the equator, rises due east only at the spring and fall equinoxes—about March 21 and September 23. It sets due west when it rises due east.

At the North Pole, where there is six months of continuous daylight, the sun is never more than 23½ degrees above the horizon.

At the equinoxes, the noon shadow of a person in Lat. 45° N. or Lat. 45° S. is exactly as long as the person is tall.

If you went from the farthest south suburb of Chicago to the one farthest north, you would have changed your latitude by more than half a degree.

If your home is exactly halfway between the North Pole and the equator, it may be in Oregon, Idaho, Montana, South Dakota, Minnesota, Wisconsin, Michigan, New Hampshire, or Maine in the United States. It may be in southern Canada. In Europe it may be in France, Italy, Yugoslavia, Rumania, or the U.S.S.R. In Asia it may be in the U.S.S.R., Mongolia, Manchuria, or at the very northern tip of Japan.

If you live halfway between the equator and the South Pole, your home must be in Argentina, Chile, or New Zealand.

The southernmost town in the world is Punta Arenas, in southern Chile.

The northernmost town in the world is Etah, Greenland.

If from Shanghai, China, you could dig a hole straight through the center of the earth, you would come out not far from Buenos Aires in Argentina.

If you could dig a hole straight through the center of the earth from New York, you would come out in the Indian Ocean west of Australia.

Rome and Madrid are almost due east of Chicago.

If you traveled due east from New Orleans, you would reach Cairo in Egypt and come close to Shanghai in China.

The great cities of London, Berlin, Moscow, Leningrad, Copenhagen, Amsterdam, Rotterdam, Hamburg, Glasgow, Oslo, and Stockholm are all farther north than any part of the United States except Alaska.

Going straight south from Miami, Florida, you would touch only the western coast of South America. Going straight south from New Orleans, you would miss South America altogether.

If you traveled straight south from Los Angeles, you would reach no land till you came to Antarctica.

If you traveled straight north from Los Angeles, you would have a land route almost all the way to the North Pole. You would cross from south to north: western Nevada, eastern Oregon, eastern Washington, and western Canada.

If you traveled straight west from Los Angeles, the first land you would reach would be one of the islands of Japan.

If you traveled straight north from Belem, near the mouth of the Amazon, you would reach no land till you came to Greenland.

It is possible to sail all the way around the world along the parallel 60° S. Your journey would be half as long as a trip around the world on the equator. It would be roughly as long as a trip from the South Pole to the North Pole along a meridian. It would also be as long as a trip around the world at Lat. 60° N.

The meridian 170° W. reaches from the North Pole almost to the South Pole without hitting any land except some of the small Pacific islands.

The International Date Line, which follows the 180th meridian most of the way, avoids all large land areas.

All these 19 countries of Europe together do not take up quite as much space on the earth as Alaska: Albania, Andorra, Austria, Belgium, Britain, Bulgaria, Denmark, Greece, Hungary, Ireland, Liechtenstein, Luxembourg, Monaco, the Netherlands, Portugal, Rumania, San Marino, Switzerland, and Vatican City.

Alaska is so big that there is room in it for nearly 500 Rhode Islands.

The world's super-giant country, the U.S.S.R., is larger than the continent of South America.

Asia could hold both North and South America with room to spare.

In the world's largest city, Tokyo, there are almost as many people as there are in the whole continent of Australia.

Europe is by far the most densely populated continent. With the exception of tiny Monaco, the Netherlands has more people per square mile than any other country in the world.

EXTENT OF LAND AND WATER ON THE EARTH'S SURFACE

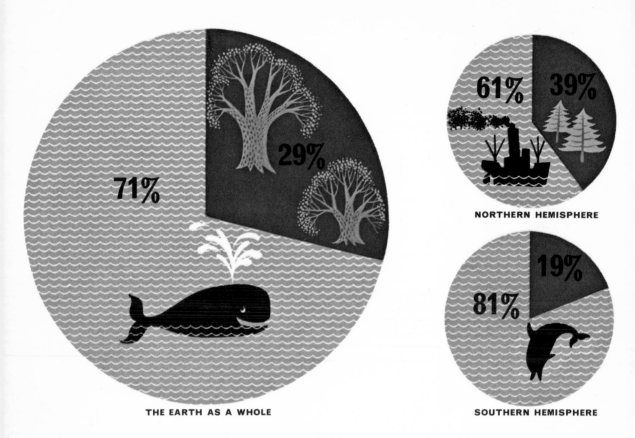

71% **29%**

THE EARTH AS A WHOLE

61% **39%**

NORTHERN HEMISPHERE

81% **19%**

SOUTHERN HEMISPHERE

THE SEVEN CONTINENTS

CONTINENT	AREA IN SQ. MI. (ROUND NUMBERS)	POPULATION (ROUND NUMBERS)
Asia	17,000,000	1,665,000,000
Africa	11,500,000	244,000,000
North America	9,300,000	265,000,000
South America	6,800,000	140,000,000
Antarctica	5,300,000	0
Europe	3,850,000	560,000,000
Australia	3,000,000	10,000,000

(Comparative Sizes)

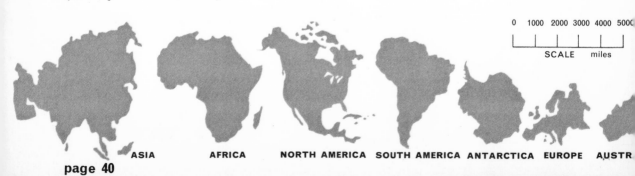

0 1000 2000 3000 4000 5000

SCALE   miles

ASIA   AFRICA   NORTH AMERICA   SOUTH AMERICA   ANTARCTICA   EUROPE   AUSTR

THE WORLD'S LARGEST ISLANDS

ISLAND	OCEAN	AREA IN SQ. MI. (ROUND NUMBERS)	POPULATION (ROUND NUMBERS)
Greenland	Arctic	840,000	31,000
New Guinea	Pacific	340,000	2,560,000
Borneo	Pacific	290,000	3,900,000
Madagascar	Indian	228,000	5,184,000
Baffin Island	Arctic	198,000	3,000
Sumatra	Indian	164,000	14,600,000
Honshu, Japan	Pacific	90,000	71,354,000
Great Britain	Atlantic	90,000	51,250,000
Victoria	Arctic	80,000	42,000
Ellesmere	Arctic	77,000	60
Celebes	Indian	73,000	6,206,000
South Island, New Zealand	Pacific	58,000	728,000
Java	Pacific	49,000	60,909,000
Cuba	Atlantic	44,000	6,743,000
North Island, New Zealand	Pacific	44,000	1,642,000
Newfoundland	Atlantic	43,000	468,000
Luzon, Philippine Islands	Pacific	41,000	7,500,000
Iceland	Atlantic	40,000	176,000
Mindanao, Philippine Islands	Pacific	37,000	1,900,000
Hokkaido, Japan	Pacific	34,000	5,039,000
Ireland	Atlantic	32,000	4,259,000
Hispaniola	Atlantic	30,000	6,519,000
Tasmania	Pacific	26,000	360,000
Banks	Arctic	26,000	0
Ceylon	Indian	25,000	9,612,000

THE EIGHT LARGEST ISLANDS
(Comparative Sizes)

0   200   400   600   800   1000
SCALE   miles

GREENLAND   NEW GUINEA   BORNEO   MADAGASCAR   BAFFIN ISLAND   SUMATRA   HONSHU   GREAT BRITAIN

THE SEVEN SEAS

Much has been written about the Seven Seas. There are only four oceans. To bring the count up to seven, the Atlantic must be divided into the North Atlantic and the South Atlantic, the Pacific must be divided into the North Pacific and the South Pacific, and the waters surrounding Antarctica must be called an ocean. Geographers used to name the Antarctic Ocean on maps, but now they seldom do so because there is no real boundary line between the waters surrounding Antarctica and the Atlantic, Pacific, and Indian oceans.

In ancient times people spoke of seven seas, too, but their seven seas were bodies of water in the Old World. They were the Mediterranean Sea, the Red Sea, the Persian Gulf, the China Sea, the Indian Ocean, the East African Ocean, and the West African Ocean.

OCEAN	Area (in sq. mi.)	Average Depth (in ft.)	Greatest Depth (in ft.)
PACIFIC	63,800,000	14,050	36,198
ATLANTIC	31,830,000	12,880	30,246
INDIAN	28,357,000	13,000	24,440
ARCTIC	5,440,000	4,200	17,850

SEA TREASURE

The oceans are a great storehouse of food. Fishermen take about 60 billion pounds of fish each year from them. Vast amounts of shellfish are caught, too. And the algae growing in the "pastures of the sea" are a possible future source of food.

Whales, seals, and walruses furnish food, but whales are also valuable for their oil and whalebone, seals for their fur, and walruses for the ivory of their tusks. Sponges are gathered from the floors of warm seas. Pearls and precious coral come from warm seas, too.

The seas are very rich in chemicals. In every cubic mile of ocean water there are about 175 million tons, worth about 5 billion dollars. Most abundant, of course, is salt. Among the many other chemicals are compounds of magnesium, sulfur, calcium, potassium, iron, copper, lead, molybdenum, silver, vanadium, nickel, mercury, and gold.

There are more than 4 million tons of magnesium in a cubic mile of ocean water. Large quantities are being removed and used.

The ocean contains 99 per cent of the world's supply of bromine. There is about one pound of bromine in 2,000 gallons of ocean water. It is being removed and used for high-test gasoline.

In all the seas together there are about 830 million tons of gold, worth, at present prices, 929 trillion dollars. If this gold were divided equally among all the people on earth, each person's share would be about 700 pounds, enough to make everyone a millionaire. But it costs more to take gold from sea water than the gold is worth. More than 5 million cubic yards of water have to be treated to get half an ounce of gold.

More minerals are constantly being deposited in the mineral "bank" of the oceans; rivers carry about 160 million tons to the sea each year.

On the ocean floor there is treasure from shipwrecked vessels. But this forms only a tiny part of the wealth of the seven seas.

FAMOUS OCEAN CROSSINGS

In 1819 the "Savannah," the first ship to use steam in crossing an ocean, made the trip from Savannah to Liverpool in 26 days. The world's first nuclear-powered merchant ship was named for this old ship.

In 1854 the clipper "James Baines" set a record by crossing the Atlantic from Boston to Liverpool in 12 days, 6 hrs.

In 1936 the dirigible "Hindenburg" flew over the Atlantic in 42 hrs., 53 min.

In 1952 the steamship "United States" crossed the Atlantic in 3 days, 10 hrs., 40 min.

In 1957 a USAF plane flew from Tokyo to Honolulu in 6 hrs., 35 min.

In 1958 the U.S. atomic-powered submarine "Nautilus" crossed the Arctic Ocean by traveling under the polar icecap. In the same year the U.S. submarine "Skate" became the first vessel to travel across the Atlantic and back under water.

In 1959 a Boeing 707 flew from New York to Shannon, Ireland, in 5 hrs., 5 min.

In 1960 the U.S. submarine "Triton" traveled all the way around the world without surfacing. The trip took 84 days.

OCEAN DEEPS

In the floors of the oceans there are deep furrows called trenches, troughs, or deeps. The deepest are in the region shown in the upper map. Deepest of all is the Marianas Trench, which goes down to 36,198 feet. It is deeper than Mount Everest, the world's highest mountain, is tall. The deepest trench in the Atlantic is the Puerto Rico Trench, which, in one place called the Milwaukee Depth, goes down to 30,246 feet. Among the other very deep trenches are:

Acapulco-Guatemala Trench, along the west coast of Mexico and Central America.

Aleutian Trench, along the Aleutian Islands.

Bartlett Deep, south of Cuba.

Cedros Trough, along the coast of Lower California.

Monaco Deep, near the Azores.

Nares Deep, southeast of Bermuda.

Peru-Chile Trench, along the west coast of South America.

Romanche Deep, in mid-Atlantic.

Tonga-Kermadee Trench, in the South Pacific, east of the Tonga Islands.

MOUNTAINS OF THE SEA

Many mountains rise from the floor of the sea. Some are volcanoes; others are folded mountains.

Down the middle of the Atlantic there is a great mountain chain longer than any mountain chain on land. It is called the Atlantic Ridge. This 10,000-mile-long mountain chain is also broad—broader than the Andes. Some of its peaks rise above the sea to form islands. The Azores are peaks of the chain. Other islands which are peaks of the Atlantic Ridge are shown on the map.

There are similar mountain ranges in the Pacific and Indian oceans, but they are not so long. Extending across the Pacific from Hawaii to the Marianas there is a range of flat-topped mountains all far below the surface. How they came to be flat-topped is a mystery.

Many of the mountains of the sea are far older than any mountains on land. Under the sea, mountains are worn down very, very slowly. They are protected there from the wind and quick changes in temperature which help tear down mountains on land.

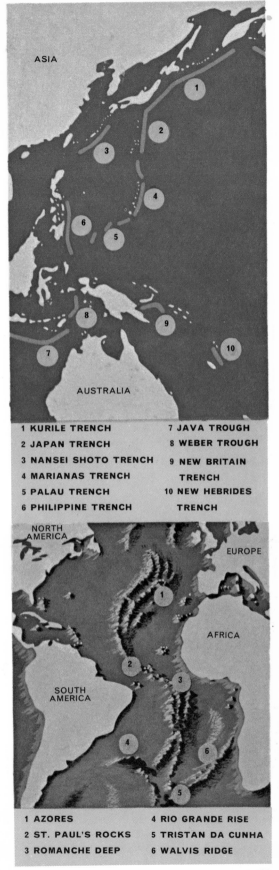

1 KURILE TRENCH	7 JAVA TROUGH
2 JAPAN TRENCH	8 WEBER TROUGH
3 NANSEI SHOTO TRENCH	9 NEW BRITAIN TRENCH
4 MARIANAS TRENCH	10 NEW HEBRIDES TRENCH
5 PALAU TRENCH	
6 PHILIPPINE TRENCH	

1 AZORES	4 RIO GRANDE RISE
2 ST. PAUL'S ROCKS	5 TRISTAN DA CUNHA
3 ROMANCHE DEEP	6 WALVIS RIDGE

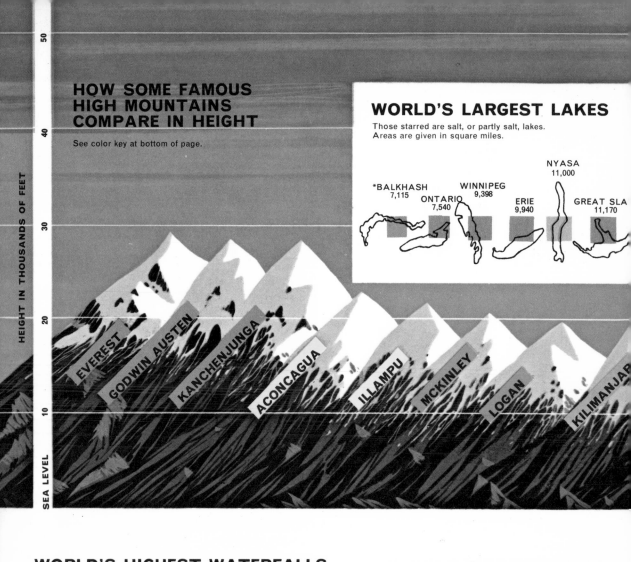

HOW SOME FAMOUS HIGH MOUNTAINS COMPARE IN HEIGHT

See color key at bottom of page.

HEIGHT IN THOUSANDS OF FEET

50
40
30
20
10
SEA LEVEL

EVEREST
GODWIN AUSTEN
KANCHENJUNGA
ACONCAGUA
ILLAMPU
MCKINLEY
LOGAN
KILIMANJARO

WORLD'S LARGEST LAKES

Those starred are salt, or partly salt, lakes.
Areas are given in square miles.

*BALKHASH
7,115

ONTARIO
7,540

WINNIPEG
9,398

ERIE
9,940

NYASA
11,000

GREAT SLA
11,170

WORLD'S HIGHEST WATERFALLS

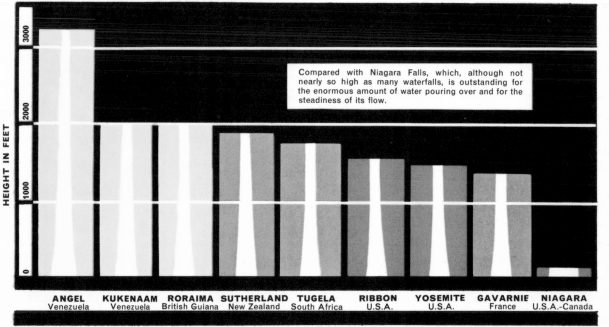

HEIGHT IN FEET

3000
2000
1000
0

Compared with Niagara Falls, which, although not nearly so high as many waterfalls, is outstanding for the enormous amount of water pouring over and for the steadiness of its flow.

ANGEL	KUKENAAM	RORAIMA	SUTHERLAND	TUGELA	RIBBON	YOSEMITE	GAVARNIE	NIAGARA
Venezuela	Venezuela	British Guiana	New Zealand	South Africa	U.S.A.	U.S.A.	France	U.S.A.-Canada

COLOR KEY:

 AFRICA   ANTARCTICA   ASIA   AUSTRALIA

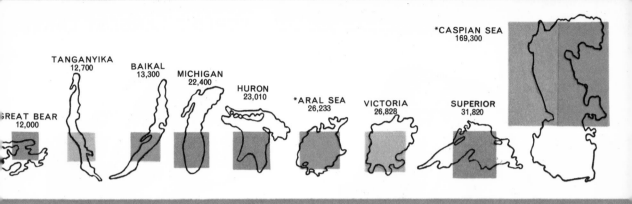

GREAT BEAR
12,000

TANGANYIKA
12,700

BAIKAL
13,300

MICHIGAN
22,400

HURON
23,010

*ARAL SEA
26,233

VICTORIA
26,828

SUPERIOR
31,820

*CASPIAN SEA
169,300

...AXI

ORIZABA

ELBRUS

KENYA

RUWENZORI

MONT BLANC

MARKHAM

MATTERHORN

EREBUS

KOSCIUSKO

WORLD'S LONGEST RIVERS

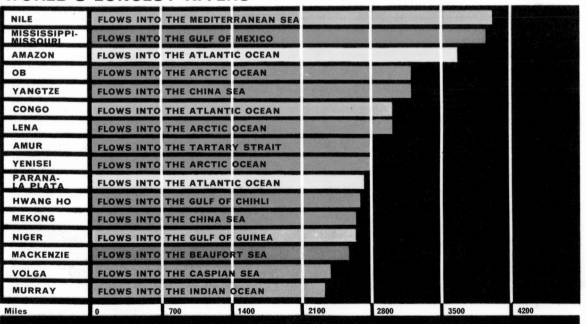

NILE	FLOWS INTO THE MEDITERRANEAN SEA						
MISSISSIPPI-MISSOURI	FLOWS INTO THE GULF OF MEXICO						
AMAZON	FLOWS INTO THE ATLANTIC OCEAN						
OB	FLOWS INTO THE ARCTIC OCEAN						
YANGTZE	FLOWS INTO THE CHINA SEA						
CONGO	FLOWS INTO THE ATLANTIC OCEAN						
LENA	FLOWS INTO THE ARCTIC OCEAN						
AMUR	FLOWS INTO THE TARTARY STRAIT						
YENISEI	FLOWS INTO THE ARCTIC OCEAN						
PARANA-LA PLATA	FLOWS INTO THE ATLANTIC OCEAN						
HWANG HO	FLOWS INTO THE GULF OF CHIHLI						
MEKONG	FLOWS INTO THE CHINA SEA						
NIGER	FLOWS INTO THE GULF OF GUINEA						
MACKENZIE	FLOWS INTO THE BEAUFORT SEA						
VOLGA	FLOWS INTO THE CASPIAN SEA						
MURRAY	FLOWS INTO THE INDIAN OCEAN						
Miles	0	700	1400	2100	2800	3500	4200

 EUROPE

 NEW ZEALAND

 NORTH AMERICA

 SOUTH AMERICA

MOUNTAIN BUILDING

Many people believe that the earth's present mountains have always been where they are. This idea is wrong. Different times in the earth's history have been mountain-building periods. The diagrams below show ways in which mountains may be made.

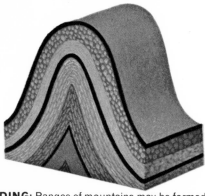

FOLDING: Ranges of mountains may be formed by the pushing up of surface layers of rock into great folds.

INTRUSIONS OF MAGMA: A single mountain may be pushed up by magma, or hot liquid rock, from deep inside the earth.

FAULTING: Ranges of mountains may be formed by the slipping of masses of rock along great cracks.

VOLCANIC ERUPTION: A single mountain may be a volcano, a mountain built up by a volcanic eruption.

RIVERS AND THEIR VALLEYS

Rivers are the great enemies of mountains and other highlands. They, armed with sand and pebbles, wear away the rocks of which the highlands are made. They carve valleys, which they gradually deepen and widen. The wearing away of land is called erosion.

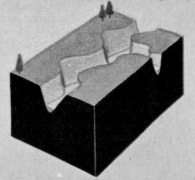
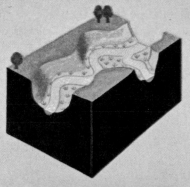
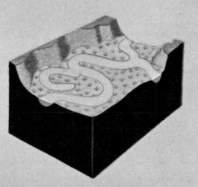

EARTH HISTORY

The earth has had a very long history. No one knows exactly how old the earth is, but most scientists agree it is at least 4 billion years old.

A very great deal of the earth's long history can be read only from the earth's rocks. Different kinds of rock tell different stories. The arrangements of rocks also help tell the earth's history. Fossils, traces found in rocks of the living things of long ago, help, too.

Let us suppose that the earth is just 4 billion years old and that a book has been written with a page to represent every million years in the earth's existence. The book has 4,000 pages. Let us suppose that there are 100 lines on each page with 10 words to each line. Each line stands for 10,000 years and each word for 1,000 years.

In this book the appearance of man on the earth would be somewhere on page 3999. The more than 4,500 years since the building of the pyramids in Egypt would be represented by the last half of the last line on page 4000. And the nearly five centuries since Columbus reached America would be represented by the last half of the last word in the last line!

Scientists have divided the history of the earth into eras. They have divided the eras, except for the very earliest, into periods and the periods into epochs. The chart that follows tells the story of North America.

NORTH AMERICA'S DIARY

	PERIOD	EVENTS	LIFE
AZOIC	2 billion years or more	Earth "born." Earliest rocks formed. Continents and oceans defined.	No life.
ARCHEOZOIC	KEEWATIN 800 million years TEMISKAMING 300 million years	Great volcanic activity. Mountains pushed up in what is now Canada. Parts of North America covered with shallow seas from time to time. First sedimentary rocks formed.	Very simple one-celled plants and animals probably present. At least blue-green algae by end of era.
PROTEROZOIC	HURONIAN 250 million years KEWEENAWAN 250 million years	Many sedimentary rocks formed. Earliest known glaciers. Volcanic activity in eastern and central North America. Great mountains pushed up in Great Lakes region and then worn down completely.	Sponges and many other invertebrates probably common. Many seaweeds.

EVENTS	LIFE

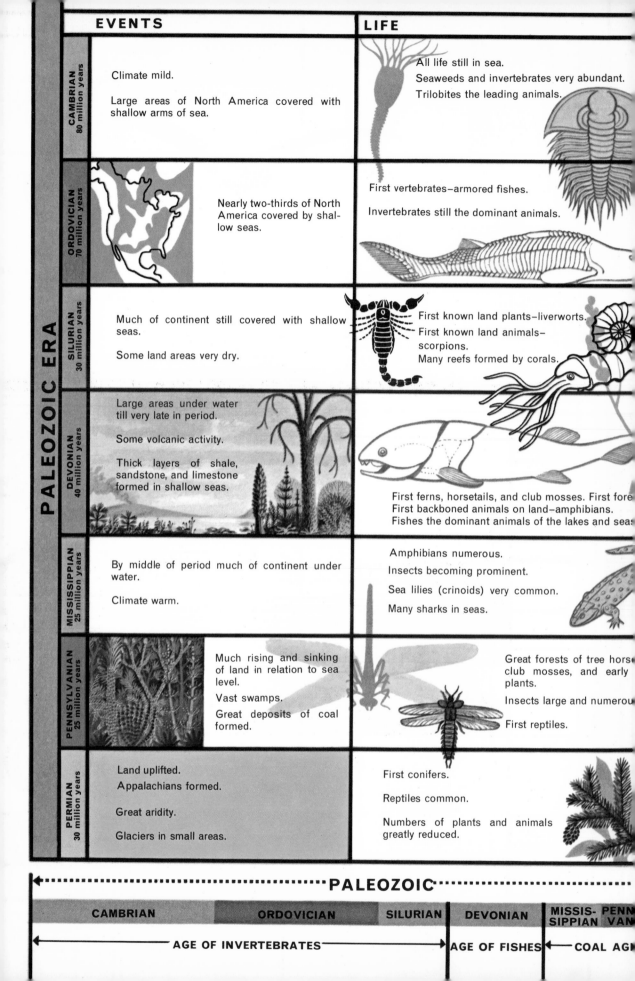

PALEOZOIC ERA

CAMBRIAN — 80 million years

Climate mild.

Large areas of North America covered with shallow arms of sea.

All life still in sea.
Seaweeds and invertebrates very abundant.
Trilobites the leading animals.

ORDOVICIAN — 70 million years

Nearly two-thirds of North America covered by shallow seas.

First vertebrates–armored fishes.

Invertebrates still the dominant animals.

SILURIAN — 30 million years

Much of continent still covered with shallow seas.

Some land areas very dry.

First known land plants–liverworts.
First known land animals–scorpions.
Many reefs formed by corals.

DEVONIAN — 40 million years

Large areas under water till very late in period.

Some volcanic activity.

Thick layers of shale, sandstone, and limestone formed in shallow seas.

First ferns, horsetails, and club mosses. First fore
First backboned animals on land–amphibians.
Fishes the dominant animals of the lakes and seas

MISSISSIPPIAN — 25 million years

By middle of period much of continent under water.

Climate warm.

Amphibians numerous.
Insects becoming prominent.
Sea lilies (crinoids) very common.
Many sharks in seas.

PENNSYLVANIAN — 25 million years

Much rising and sinking of land in relation to sea level.

Vast swamps.

Great deposits of coal formed.

Great forests of tree hors
club mosses, and early plants.
Insects large and numerou
First reptiles.

PERMIAN — 30 million years

Land uplifted.
Appalachians formed.

Great aridity.

Glaciers in small areas.

First conifers.

Reptiles common.

Numbers of plants and animals greatly reduced.

PALEOZOIC

CAMBRIAN	ORDOVICIAN	SILURIAN	DEVONIAN	MISSIS-SIPPIAN	PENN VAN

AGE OF INVERTEBRATES ——————— AGE OF FISHES ◄— COAL AG

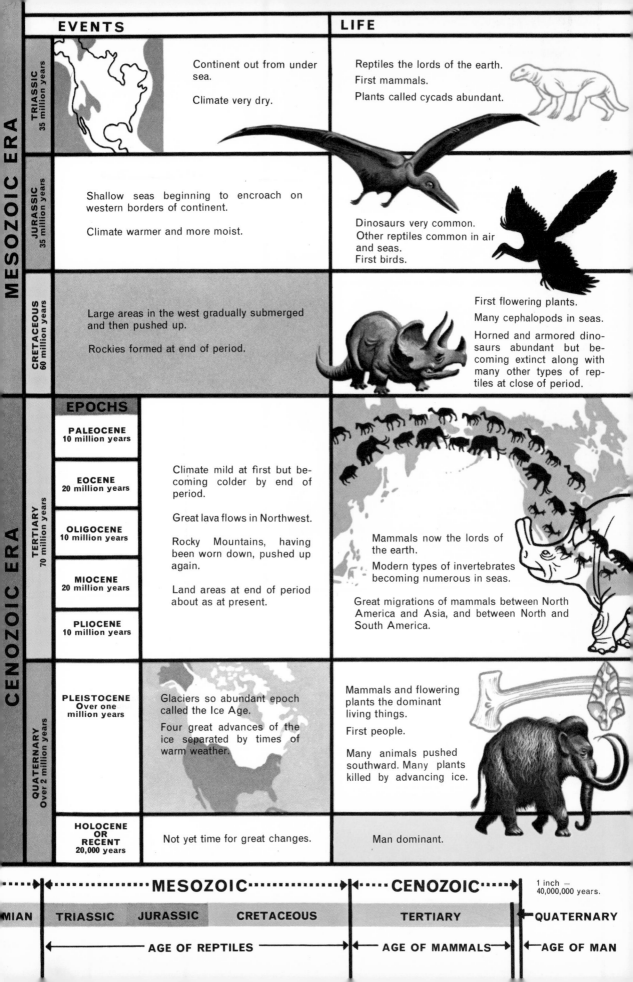

EVENTS	LIFE

MESOZOIC ERA

TRIASSIC — 35 million years

EVENTS: Continent out from under sea. Climate very dry.

LIFE: Reptiles the lords of the earth. First mammals. Plants called cycads abundant.

JURASSIC — 35 million years

EVENTS: Shallow seas beginning to encroach on western borders of continent. Climate warmer and more moist.

LIFE: Dinosaurs very common. Other reptiles common in air and seas. First birds.

CRETACEOUS — 60 million years

EVENTS: Large areas in the west gradually submerged and then pushed up. Rockies formed at end of period.

LIFE: First flowering plants. Many cephalopods in seas. Horned and armored dinosaurs abundant but becoming extinct along with many other types of reptiles at close of period.

CENOZOIC ERA

TERTIARY — 70 million years

EPOCHS

- PALEOCENE — 10 million years
- EOCENE — 20 million years
- OLIGOCENE — 10 million years
- MIOCENE — 20 million years
- PLIOCENE — 10 million years

EVENTS: Climate mild at first but becoming colder by end of period. Great lava flows in Northwest. Rocky Mountains, having been worn down, pushed up again. Land areas at end of period about as at present.

LIFE: Mammals now the lords of the earth. Modern types of invertebrates becoming numerous in seas. Great migrations of mammals between North America and Asia, and between North and South America.

QUATERNARY — Over 2 million years

- PLEISTOCENE — Over one million years

EVENTS: Glaciers so abundant epoch called the Ice Age. Four great advances of the ice separated by times of warm weather.

LIFE: Mammals and flowering plants the dominant living things. First people. Many animals pushed southward. Many plants killed by advancing ice.

- HOLOCENE OR RECENT — 20,000 years

EVENTS: Not yet time for great changes.

LIFE: Man dominant.

MESOZOIC · · · · · · · · ▶ CENOZOIC · · · ·

1 inch = 40,000,000 years.

| MIAN | TRIASSIC | JURASSIC | CRETACEOUS | TERTIARY | QUATERNARY |

◀— AGE OF REPTILES —▶ ◀— AGE OF MAMMALS —▶ ◀— AGE OF MAN

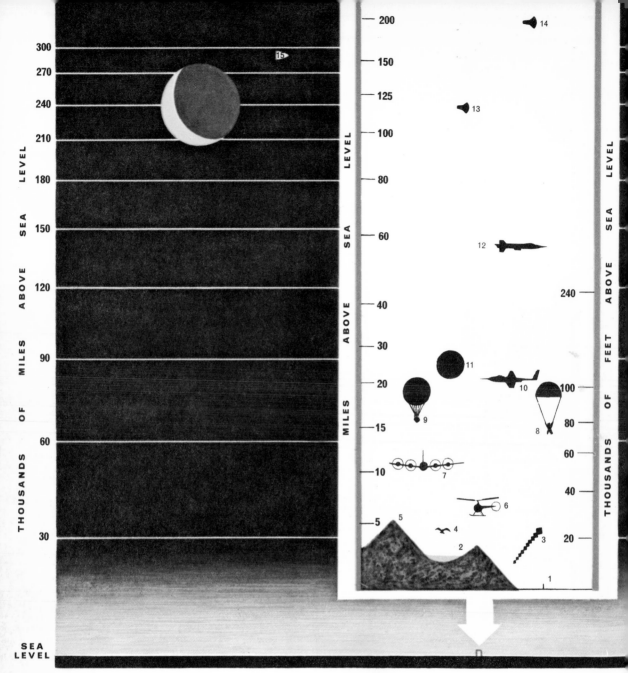

RECORD HIGHS

1. Highest structure built by man—television tower, Cape Girardeau, Mo. 1,676 ft.
2. Highest lake—Lake Titicaca . . 12,507 ft.
3. Highest kite (ten kites in tandem) ascent . . . . 23,385 ft.
4. Highest altitude at which birds have been seen to fly . . . . 26,000 ft.
5. Highest mountain peak—Mount Everest . . . . 29,141 ft.
6. Highest helicopter ascent . . . . 36,037 ft.
7. Highest propeller plane ascent 56,046 ft.
8. Highest parachute jump . . . . 102,800 ft.

9. Highest manned balloon ascent 113,500 ft.
10. Highest jet plane ascent . . . . 113,891 ft.
11. Highest unmanned balloon ascent 138,000 ft.
12. Highest rocket plane ascent . . . 59.61 mi.
13. Highest point reached by manned satellite in non-orbital flight . . . . 118 mi.
14. Highest point reached by manned satellite in orbit . . . . 187.65 mi.
15. Farthest point reached by earth satellite (Lunik III) . . . . 292,000 mi.

RECORD LOWS

1. Depth reached by skin diver with aqualung .... 397 ft.
2. Depth to which diver in full flexible diving suit can go ...... 728 ft.
3. Deepest level for submarines Over 800 ft. (Record is classified information.)
4. Lowest point on continents— Dead Sea ...... 1,286 ft. below sea level
5. Depth to which whales can dive 3,000 ft.
6. Deepest descent of bathysphere 3,028 ft.
7. Deepest descent of benthyscope 4,500 ft.
8. Depth to which sunlight can penetrate .... 5,000 ft.
9. Deepest well for water (near Blackall, Queensland, Australia) 7,009 ft.
10. Deepest mine (gold mine, Kolar, India) .... 10,030 ft.
11. Deepest oil well (Texas) ..... 25,340 ft.
12. Deepest descent of bathyscaphe 35,800 ft.
13. Deepest level at which animal life has been found .... 35,800 ft.
14. Deepest ocean depth (Marianas Trench, Pacific Ocean) ...... 36,198 ft.

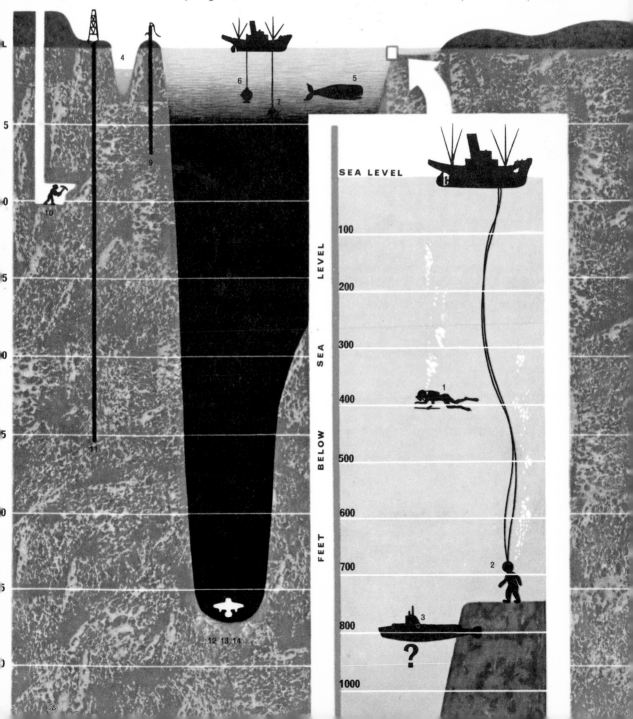

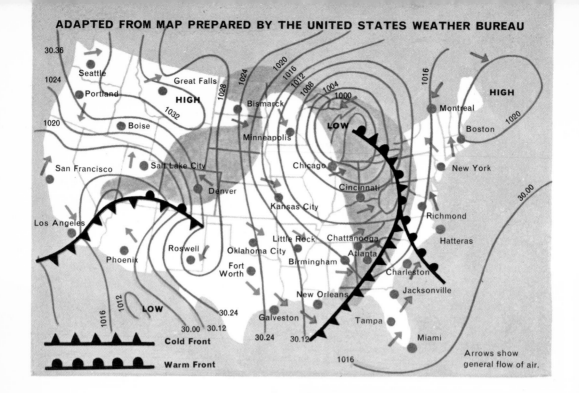

30.36

1024 Seattle

Great Falls

Portland

HIGH

Boise

1020

San Francisco

Salt Lake City

Denver

Los Angeles

Roswell

Phoenix

Fort Worth

LOW

30.24

30.00 30.12

Galveston

30.24 30.12

Bismarck

Minneapolis

Chicago

Kansas City

Oklahoma City

Little Rock

Birmingham

New Orleans

LOW

Cincinnati

Chattanooga

Atlanta

Tampa

Montreal

HIGH

Boston

New York

Richmond

Hatteras

Charleston

Jacksonville

Miami

1016

Arrows show
general flow of air.

▲▲▲▲▲ **Cold Front**

●●●● **Warm Front**

WEATHER TERMS

AIR PRESSURE The force with which the air pushes down. Winds are caused by differences in air pressure.

ANTICYCLONE The movement of air outward from the center of an area of high pressure.

BLIZZARD A snowstorm with a strong wind.

CEILING The height of the base of any clouds which are lower than 9,750 feet and which cover more than half the sky. If there is a heavy fog resting on the ground, the ceiling is zero. If there are no clouds in sight, or if the clouds are above 9,750 feet, the ceiling is "unlimited."

CLIMATE Average weather conditions over a long period.

CLOUDBURST A storm in which a very heavy rain falls in a short time.

CLOUD SEEDING The dropping of crystals of sodium iodide or some similar chemical on clouds to make them drop some of their moisture.

COLD FRONT The boundary between a mass of cool or cold air and one of warmer air at which the cooler air is pushing its way under the warmer air.

COLD WAVE Cold weather that lasts for several days.

CONDENSATION The changing of water vapor to water or ice.

CYCLONE The movement of air in toward the center of an area of low pressure.

DEW Drops of water that form on objects from the condensation of water vapor in the air. Dew does not fall; it is formed where you find it.

DUST STORM A storm in which strong winds carry great amounts of dry topsoil.

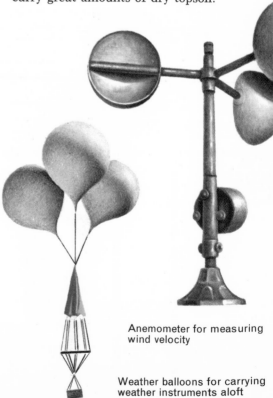

Anemometer for measuring wind velocity

Weather balloons for carrying weather instruments aloft

Fog   A cloud close to the ground, made up of very tiny droplets of water.

Frost   Crystals of ice that form on objects from the condensation of water vapor in the air. Frost, like dew, is formed where you find it.

Glaze   A coating of ice formed when rain freezes on the surfaces it strikes; e.g., on the branches of trees and bushes.

Hail   Balls made up of layers of ice and snow, formed when raindrops freeze high above the earth and move up and down in the clouds before they fall to the ground.

High   The movement of air outward from a region of high air pressure; an anticyclone.

Humidity   The amount of water vapor in the air.

Hurricane   A great windstorm covering hundreds of square miles and often lasting a whole day. Hurricanes originate in warm regions over the oceans. They are often called "tropical cyclones."

Ice Storm   A storm in which glaze forms on the branches of trees, telephone wires, bushes, and other such objects. Often the weight of the ice does much damage.

Isobar   A line on a weather map joining places of the same air pressure.

Isotherm   A dotted line on a weather map connecting places with the same temperature.

Jet Stream   A swiftly moving current of air some 400 miles wide and 4 miles deep, and from 20,000 to 40,000 feet above the ground. The speed of the air in a jet stream may reach 250 miles an hour. Airplanes often take advantage of a jet stream to increase their speed.

Low   The movement of air inward toward the center of an area of low air pressure; a cyclone.

Millibar   A unit of pressure. On weather maps the air pressure may be marked in both inches (the height of the mercury in a mercury barometer) and millibars.

Precipitation   Condensed moisture that falls from clouds: rain, snow, sleet, or hail.

Relative Humidity   The amount of water vapor in the air in comparison with the amount that the air might contain.

Sleet   Small balls of ice formed when rain freezes as it falls.

Smog   A combination of smoke and fog.

Stationary Front   A cold front or warm front that has slowed down its eastward movement almost to a standstill.

Temperature-Humidity Index   A figure taking into account both the temperature and the humidity at a given time. Very few people are uncomfortable because of the heat and humidity if the index figure is 70 or below. Many are uncomfortable if it reaches 75. And almost everyone is uncomfortable if the index climbs to 79 or above.

Thunderstorm   A local storm in which there is much thunder and lightning.

Tornado   A very violent windstorm covering only a small area and moving very fast; often wrongly called a "cyclone."

Typhoon   The name given to a hurricane that originates over the Pacific Ocean.

Unsettled Weather   Changeable weather with a strong possibility of rain or snow.

Warm Front   A boundary between a mass of warm air and a mass of cooler air at which the warm air is climbing up over the cooler air.

Weather Map   A map showing weather conditions over a large area and forming a basis for weather predictions.

Wind Direction   The direction *from* which the wind is blowing.

Wind Velocity   The speed of wind measured in miles per hour or in knots.

TERMS USED IN U. S. WEATHER BUREAU FORECASTS	MILES PER HOUR	WIND EFFECTS OBSERVED ON LAND
LIGHT	less than 1 1-3 4-7	calm; smoke rises vertically direction of wind shown by smoke drift, but not by wind vanes wind felt on face; leaves rustle; ordinary vane moved by wind
GENTLE	8-12	leaves and small twigs in constant motion; wind extends light flag
MODERATE	13-18	raises dust, loose paper; small branches are moved
FRESH	19-24	small trees in leaf begin to sway; crested wavelets form on inland waters
STRONG	25-31 32-38	large branches in motion; whistling heard in telegraph wires; umbrellas used with difficulty whole trees in motion; inconvenience felt walking against wind
GALE	39-46 47-54	breaks twigs off trees; generally impedes progress slight structural damage occurs (chimney pots, slates removed)
WHOLE GALE	55-63 64-74	seldom experienced inland; trees uprooted; considerable structural damage occurs rarely experienced; accompanied by widespread damage
HURRICANE	75 or more	very rarely experienced; widespread damage

Ten inches of snow contain roughly the same amount of water as one inch of rain. An inch of rain is the amount of rain that would make a layer an inch deep on level ground if none ran off or sank in.

HYGROGRAPH
(records humidity)

SLING PSYCHROMETER
(measures relative humidity)

TIPPING BUCKET RAIN GAUG
(measures rainfall)

PRECIPITATION RECORDS

Heaviest rainfall recorded in one minute—1.23 inches—Unionville, Md.—July 4, 1956

Heaviest rainfall recorded in one hour—12 inches—Holt, Mo.—June 22, 1947

Heaviest rainfall recorded in 24 hours—46 inches—Baguio, Luzon, P. I.—July 14/15, 1911

Heaviest rainfall recorded in one month—366.14 inches—Cherrapunji, India—July, 1861

World's highest average annual rainfall—471.68 inches—Mt. Waialeale, Hawaii

World's lowest average annual rainfall—.02 inch—Arica, Chile

Lowest average annual rainfall in the U.S.—1.66 inches—Greenland Ranch, Calif.

Longest dry spell recorded in the U.S.—767 days—Bagdad, Calif.—Oct. 3, 1912 –Nov. 8, 1914

Heaviest snowfall in 24 hours in the U.S.—76 inches—Silver Lake, Colo.—April 14/15, 1921

Heaviest snowfall in one month in the U.S.—390 inches—Tamarack, Calif.—January, 1911

Heaviest snowfall in one season in the U.S.—1000.3 inches—Paradise Ranger Station, Mt. Rainier, Wash.—1955/56

Greatest average annual snowfall in the U.S.—575.1 inches—Paradise Ranger Station, Mt. Rainier, Wash.

Largest recorded hailstone in the U.S.—17 inches in circumference, weight 1½ pounds—Potter, Neb.—July 6, 1928

AVERAGE PRECIPITATION

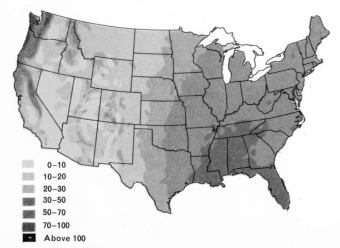

0–10
10–20
20–30
30–50
50–70
70–100
Above 100

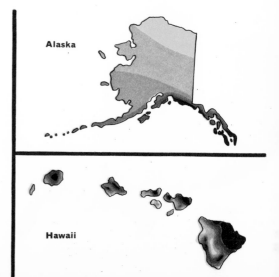

Alaska

Hawaii

ANEROID BAROMETER

MAXIMUM AND MINIMUM THERMOMETER

ALCOHOL THERMOMETER

This diagram shows how Fahrenheit and centigrade readings compare. To change centigrade to Fahrenheit, multiply by 1.8 and add 32 degrees. To change Fahrenheit to centigrade, subtract 32 degrees and divide by 1.8.

RECORDING THERMOMETER

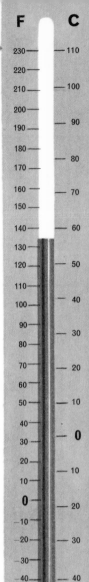

TEMPERATURE RECORDS

Highest temperature recorded anywhere in world	136°F. Azizia, Libya	Sept. 13, 1922
Highest temperature recorded in the United States	134°F. Death Valley, Calif.	July 10, 1913
Highest average annual temperature in the world	88°F. Lugh, Somaliland	
Highest average annual temperature in the U.S.	77.6°F. Key West, Florida	
Lowest temperature recorded anywhere in world	−125.3°F. Vostok, Antarctica	Aug. 25, 1958
Lowest temperature recorded in northern hemisphere	−89.9°F. Oimekon, Siberia	Feb. 1, 1933
Lowest temperature recorded in the United States	−70°F. Rogers Pass, Mont.	Jan. 20, 1954
Lowest average annual temperature in the world	−71°F. Sovietskaya, near South Pole	
Lowest average annual temperature in the U.S.	10.1°F. Barrow, Alaska	

AVERAGE TEMPERATURE

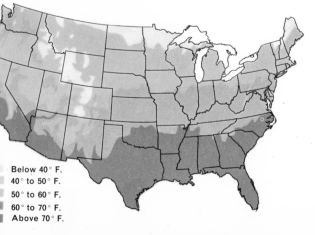

Below 40° F.
40° to 50° F.
50° to 60° F.
60° to 70° F.
Above 70° F.

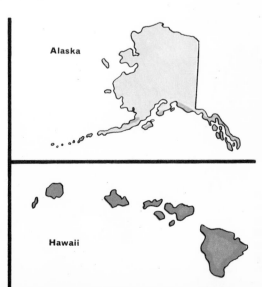

Alaska

Hawaii

NINE CLOUD TYPES

CIRRUS
Delicate wispy white clouds always made of ice crystals. Before sunrise and after sunset, often colored yellow or red. Average height above ground 25,000 feet.

CIRROSTRATUS
Thin white clouds forming a gauzy veil that causes halos around the sun and moon. Never thick enough to prevent shadows. Average height 20,000 feet.

CIRROCUMULUS
Small white flakes of clouds forming an even pattern. Sky covered with clouds of this kind often called mackerel sky. Average height 20,000 feet.

CUMULUS
Fluffy towering white clouds with rounded tops and flat bases. Often called fair-weather clouds. Average height of base 1,600 feet. Average height of top 10,000 feet.

CUMULONIMBUS
Towering clouds, often anvil-topped, popularly called thunderheads. May bring heavy showers and hail. Average height of base 1,600 feet, of top 25,000 feet.

ALTOCUMULUS
White or gray clouds forming broken-up layers or patches somewhat like the cirrocumulus clouds of a mackerel sky. Average height of base 6,500 feet.

STRATUS
Grayish clouds forming a uniform layer. Like fog but not resting on ground. May produce drizzle. Height of base from near ground to 6,500 feet.

STRATOCUMULUS
Dull gray clouds forming a layer broken up into large lumpy masses or long rolls. May give wavy look to sky. Height of base from near surface of ground to 6,500 feet.

NIMBOSTRATUS
Dark gray clouds forming a nearly uniform layer over sky. True rain clouds. Bring snow in winter. Height of base from near ground to 6,500 feet.

STORMS

TORNADOES
Tornadoes occur most often in the spring and early summer months. Tornado winds are the strongest winds known.

HURRICANES
Hurricanes, called typhoons in the lands bordering the Pacific, occur most often in late summer and early fall.

THUNDERSTORMS
Thunderstorms are chiefly summer storms. Most common U.S. storms, they may be dry but often bring rain or hail.

ICE STORMS
Ice storms occur most often in late fall and early spring, when it is just cold enough for raindrops to freeze as they strike.

BLIZZARDS
Blizzards are winter storms. They are snowstorms with winds strong enough to pile the snow into big drifts.

DUST STORMS
Dust storms are usually summer storms, but they may come at any time when the soil is dry enough to be blown about.

STORM AND HURRICANE WARNINGS

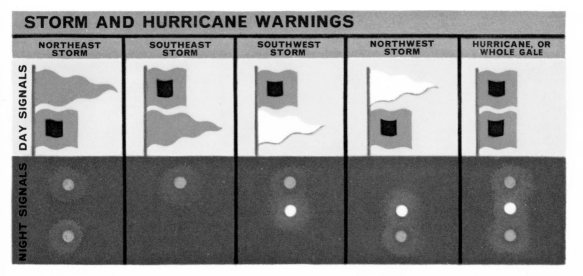

	NORTHEAST STORM	SOUTHEAST STORM	SOUTHWEST STORM	NORTHWEST STORM	HURRICANE, OR WHOLE GALE
DAY SIGNALS					
NIGHT SIGNALS					

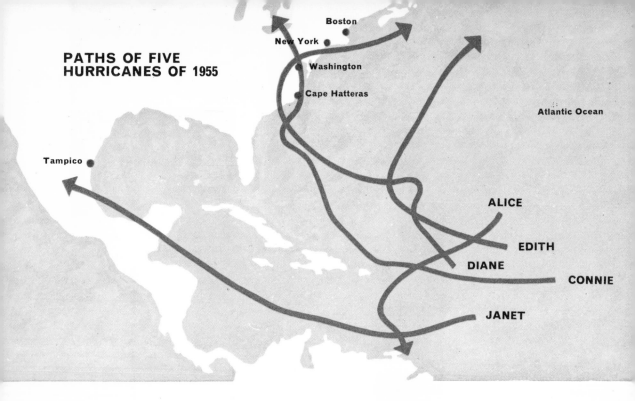

PATHS OF FIVE
HURRICANES OF 1955

Boston

New York

Washington

Cape Hatteras

Atlantic Ocean

Tampico

ALICE

EDITH

DIANE

CONNIE

JANET

HOW HURRICANES ARE NAMED

In recent years hurricanes have been given girls' names by the U. S. Weather Bureau. The first hurricane of a season is given a name that begins with A, the second a name that begins with B, and so on into the alphabet. There never has been a hurricane named Wilhelmina partly because, fortunately, there have never been enough hurricanes in a season to reach the W's in the alphabet. No names of more than two syllables, moreover, are ever chosen. Early in 1960 it was decided that the names must be selected from a list that had been compiled. The list has four names for each letter except for Q and a few others. The four A's are Abby, Anna, Alma, and Arlene. After these names have been used up in order for the first hurricanes of four years, they will be used in order again unless one of the hurricanes proves to be exceptionally disastrous. In that case the storm will keep its name and another name will be substituted in the list. The plan is the same for every letter used.

Typhoons, the hurricanes of the Pacific regions, are named as hurricanes are. Pamela was a disastrous typhoon of 1961.

HABITS OF HURRICANES

The hurricanes that strike eastern and southern United States originate as a rule in the eastern Atlantic near the Cape Verde Islands or in the Caribbean Sea near the West Indies. All hurricanes and typhoons originate in the tropics.

Hurricanes seldom move far inland.

In hurricanes, since they strike coastal areas, the danger from high waves is often greater than the danger from high winds.

Winds of as high as 186 miles an hour have been recorded in hurricanes, and it is estimated that hurricane winds sometimes reach 250 miles per hour. "Hurricane" comes from a Carib Indian word meaning "big wind."

Hurricanes are usually from 300 to 600 miles in diameter.

At the eye, or center, of a hurricane there is a calm. The eye is about 14 miles across on the average.

A hurricane moves on its course at a rate of from 10 to 60 miles an hour.

The average "life" of a hurricane is about 9 days. August hurricanes last longest—about 12 days. A hurricane lasts only a day or so in any one place.

Hurricanes often bring torrential rains.

The energy released by a hurricane in one second is as great as the energy released by several atomic bombs.

Radar has been a great help in tracking hurricanes and giving warning of their approach. At the right is a radar "portrait" of a hurricane. Weather satellites are now a help, too. Esther, the fifth hurricane of the 1961 season, was the first hurricane discovered by a satellite. It was photographed by Tiros III.

OCCURRENCE OF HURRICANES 1886-1958

Hurricanes are clearly late summer and autumn storms.

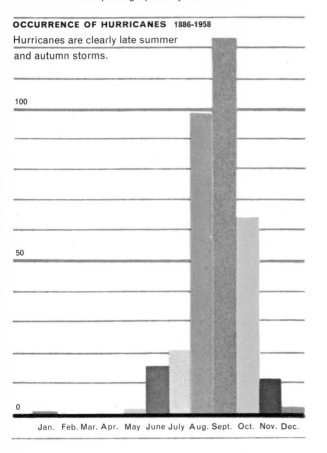

TEN DISASTROUS TROPICAL STORMS IN OTHER LANDS

DATE	COUNTRY	LIVES LOST
1906	China	10,000
1930	Dominican Republic	2,000
1934	Japan	4,000
1942	India	40,000
1949	Philippines	1,000
1953	Vietnam	1,000
1954	Japan	1,200
1955	Mexico	200
1958	Japan	600
1959	Japan	5,000

TEN DISASTROUS HURRICANES IN THE UNITED STATES

DATE	LOCALITY (Area hardest hit)	LIVES LOST	DAMAGE	NAME
Sept. 1900	Galveston, Tex.	6,000	$ 20,000,000	
Sept. 1909	New Orleans, La.	350	5,000,000	
Sept. 1928	Southern Florida	1,836	25,000,000	
Sept. 1938	Southern New England	600	250,000,000	
Aug. 1954	North Carolina to Maine	60	461,000,000	Carol
Oct. 1954	South Carolina to New York	95	252,000,000	Hazel
Aug. 1955	North Carolina to New England	184	832,000,000	Diane
June 1957	Southeast Texas and southwest Louisiana	390	150,000,000	Audrey
Sept. 1960	Puerto Rico and Florida to New England	152	Over 500,000,000	Donna
Sept. 1961	Texas and Louisiana	46	Over 300,000,000	Carla

WEATHER SAYINGS

Here are twenty common sayings about the weather. Some are well founded; others are not. Can you tell which ones are sound? After trying, you may find out whether you are weather-wise by reading the explanations at the bottom of the opposite page.

1. If the groundhog sees his shadow on groundhog day, February 2, six more weeks of cold weather are ahead.

2. If March comes in like a lion, it will go out like a lamb.

3. If it rains before seven, it will stop before eleven.

4. A red sunset means stormy weather next day.

5. Rainbow in the morning,
    sailors take warning;
   Rainbow at night,
    sailors' delight.

6. A ring around the moon means bad weather ahead.

7. When the wind is in the east, it's good for neither man nor beast.

8. If it rains on Easter Sunday, it will rain the six following Sundays.

9. A heavy dew is a sign of clear weather ahead.

10. If a crescent moon's horns are turned up "to hold water," there will be rain soon.

11. It is sometimes too cold to snow.

12. It is not the heat but the humidity that makes us very uncomfortable on hot days.

13. Dew falls at night.

14. If you hear a clap of thunder, there is no danger that you will be struck by the bolt that caused the clap.

15. Open windows attract lightning.

16. Thunder makes milk sour.

17. Lightning never strikes in the same place twice.

18. April showers bring May flowers.

19. No two snowflakes are ever exactly alike.

20. Snow is frozen rain.

TWENTY FAMOUS FLOODS

DATE	LOCATION	CAUSE	CASUALTIES AND DAMAGE
1228	Holland	Sea flood	100,000 deaths
1642	China	Seawall destroyed by rebels	300,000 deaths
1887	China (Hanan Province)	Overflow of Hwang Ho	900,000 deaths
1889	Johnstown, Pa.	Washout of dam on Conamaugh River	2,200 deaths
1896	Sanriku, Japan	Earthquake and tidal wave	27,000 deaths
1911	China	Overflow of Yangtze River	100,000 deaths
1913	Ohio and Indiana	Overflow of the rivers of the two states	732 deaths
1928	Santa Paula, Calif.	Collapse of St. Francis Dam	450 deaths
1937	Ohio and Mississippi valleys	Unusually heavy January rains: 16-20 inches in 25 days	250 deaths, 700,000 homeless, $500,000,000 property destruction
1946	Alaska and Hawaii	Tidal waves	150 deaths
1948	Turkey	Bursting of river dikes	Hundreds drowned
1950	China	Overflow of eastern and southern rivers	500 deaths and 1,000,000 homeless
1953	Northwest Europe (North Sea area)	Storm followed by floods	1,794 deaths in the Netherlands
1954	Iran	Flash flood	2,000 deaths
1954	Mexico-Texas border	Rio Grande flooded	50 deaths
1955	India and Pakistan	Overflow of rivers	1,700 deaths
1955	Oregon and northern California	Week of heavy rains	74 deaths, $150,000,000 damage
1956	Iran	Overflow of rivers	300 deaths
1957	China	Yi Shu and Hwang Ho rivers flooded	557 deaths
1959	Southern France	Collapse of Malpasset Dam	Over 500 deaths

HOW THE AVERAGE JANUARY AND JULY TEMPERATURES OF TWELVE AMERICAN CITIES COMPARE

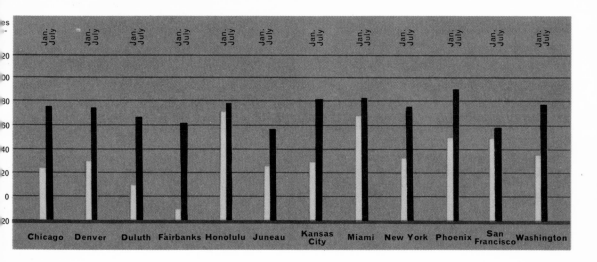

Chicago   Denver   Duluth   Fairbanks   Honolulu   Juneau   Kansas City   Miami   New York   Phoenix   San Francisco   Washington

WEATHER SAYINGS (ANSWERS)

1. False. The groundhog has no standing as a weather prophet.

2. False. But the proverb does call our attention to the fact that March is a month of changeable weather.

3. Most rains last for only a few hours. Very often a rain that starts before seven ends before eleven, but there is no assurance that it will.

4. False. Sunsets are most likely to be red when there is dry, dusty weather to the west, the direction from which our weather comes.

5. True. A rainbow in the morning must be in the west, in the opposite direction from the sun, and, to make the rainbow possible, there must be droplets of water in the air there. The wet weather will be moving on to us soon. A rainbow at night (late afternoon) must be in the east, and the sun must be shining in the west or there will be no rainbow. The fair weather to the west is in store for us.

6. True. The ring around the moon is caused by high cirrus clouds. They never bring rain or snow themselves, but they are, as a rule, the forerunners of cloudy weather.

7. True. Lows as a rule bring bad weather, and an east wind usually means the approach of a low.

8. False. Easter weather does not determine the weather that follows it.

9. True. On cloudless summer nights the earth loses its heat rapidly and dews are likely to be much heavier than on cloudy nights. Cloudless skies mean no immediate rain.

10. False. The direction the moon's horns point has to do with the position of the moon in its complicated travels, not with the weather.

11. False. A two-inch snowfall is on record at a temperature of –24° F. But cold air cannot hold as much moisture as warm air, and heavy snowfalls are therefore unlikely in very cold weather.

12. Both heat and humidity play a part in making us uncomfortable on hot days in summer. If, however, the temperature is high, we are much more uncomfortable if the humidity is also high.

13. False. Dew is formed at night, but it does not fall. It is formed where we find it.

14. True. It takes some time for the sound caused by a flash of lightning to reach us. The lightning therefore has struck before we hear the thunder.

15. False. Scientists have found no evidence for this belief.

16. False. Milk sours most easily in the kind of hot weather in which thunderstorms occur. But the thunder itself has nothing to do with the souring of the milk.

17. False. There are so many places for lightning to strike that by the laws of chance it does not often strike in the same place a second time. But there is no assurance that it will not.

18. True. May flowers often come from roots or bulbs that have lived in the ground all winter. But warmth and moisture are needed to start these roots and bulbs to growing.

19. True. Although snowflakes follow the same crystal pattern, no two snow crystals have ever been found that are exactly the same.

20. False. Snow is formed by the freezing of water vapor, not rain. Sleet is frozen rain.

THE FIFTY STATES OF THE
UNITED STATES

The State Flags of the United States

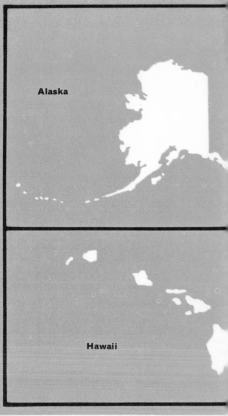

Alaska

Hawaii

Alabama

Alaska

Arizona

Arkansas

California

Colorado

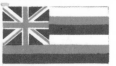

Connecticut

Delaware

Florida

Georgia

Hawaii

Idaho

Illinois

Indiana

Iowa

Kansas

Kentucky

Louisiana

Maine

Maryland

Massachusetts

Michigan

Minnesota

Mississippi

Missouri

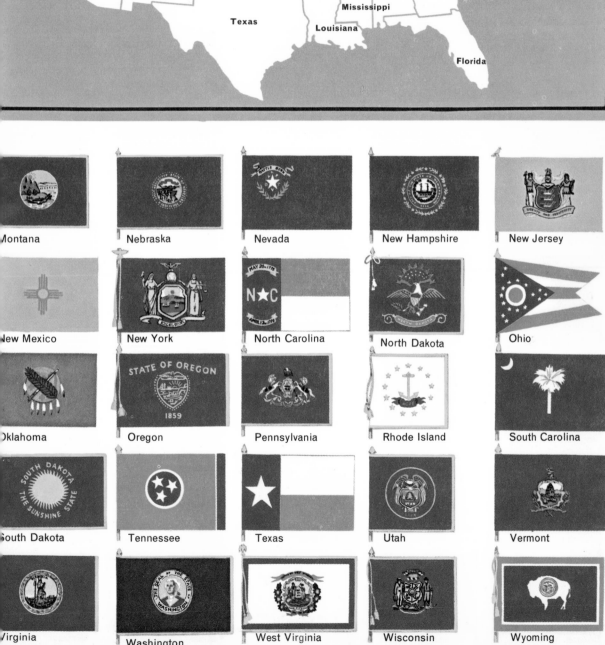

Montana	Nebraska	Nevada	New Hampshire	New Jersey
New Mexico	New York	North Carolina	North Dakota	Ohio
Oklahoma	Oregon	Pennsylvania	Rhode Island	South Carolina
South Dakota	Tennessee	Texas	Utah	Vermont
Virginia	Washington	West Virginia	Wisconsin	Wyoming

STATE	Year of Admission to Union	Order of Entry	Population (in round numbers)	Area Sq. Mi.	Area Rank	Capital	Nicknames
ALABAMA	1819	22	3,267,000	51,609	29	Montgomery	Cotton State Heart of Dixie Yellowhammer State
ALASKA	1959	49	226,000	586,400	1	Juneau	The Last Frontier
ARIZONA	1912	48	1,302,000	113,909	6	Phoenix	Sunset State Grand Canyon State
ARKANSAS	1836	25	1,786,000	53,104	27	Little Rock	Wonder State Land of Opportunity
CALIFORNIA	1850	31	15,717,000	158,693	3	Sacramento	Golden State
COLORADO	1876	38	1,754,000	104,247	8	Denver	Silver State Centennial State
CONNECTICUT	1788	5	2,535,000	5,009	48	Hartford	Nutmeg State Constitution State Land of Steady Habits
DELAWARE	1787	1	446,000	2,057	49	Dover	Blue Hen State First State Diamond State
FLORIDA	1845	27	4,952,000	58,560	22	Tallahassee	Sunshine State
GEORGIA	1788	4	3,943,000	58,876	21	Atlanta	Peach State Empire State of the Sou
HAWAII	1959	50	633,000	6,423	47	Honolulu	Aloha State Paradise of the Pacific
IDAHO	1890	43	667,000	83,557	13	Boise	Gem State Gem of the Mountains
ILLINOIS	1818	21	10,081,000	56,400	24	Springfield	Prairie State Land of Lincoln
INDIANA	1816	19	4,662,000	36,291	38	Indianapolis	Hoosier State
IOWA	1846	29	2,758,000	56,290	25	Des Moines	Hawkeye State
KANSAS	1861	34	2,179,000	82,276	14	Topeka	Sunflower State Jayhawk State Wheat State
KENTUCKY	1792	15	3,038,000	40,395	37	Frankfort	Bluegrass State
LOUISIANA	1812	18	3,257,000	48,523	31	Baton Rouge	Pelican State Creole State Sugar State
MAINE	1820	23	969,000	33,215	39	Augusta	Pine Tree State
MARYLAND	1788	7	3,101,000	10,577	42	Annapolis	Free State Old Line State
MASSACHUSETTS	1788	6	5,149,000	8,257	45	Boston	Bay State Old Colony State
MICHIGAN	1837	26	7,823,000	58,216	23	Lansing	Wolverine State
MINNESOTA	1858	32	3,414,000	84,068	12	St. Paul	Gopher State North Star State Land of 10,000 Lakes
MISSISSIPPI	1817	20	2,178,000	47,716	32	Jackson	Magnolia State

Meaning or Origin of Real Name	Songs	Colors	Mottoes	Abbreviation of State Name
"I clear the thicket"	"Alabama"	None	Audemus jura nostra defendere. (We dare defend our rights.)	Ala.
"Great country"	"Alaska's Flag"	None	None	None
"Place of the little springs"	"Arizona"	Blue and old gold	Ditat Deus. (God enriches.)	Ariz.
...me of an Indian tribe	"The Arkansas Traveler"	None	Regnat populus. (The people rule.)	Ark.
...me of a mythical island in a ...sh story written in the time ...lumbus	"I Love You, California"	Blue and gold	Eureka. (I have found it.)	Calif.
...: "Red"	"Where the Colum-bines Grow"	Blue and white	Nil sine Numine (Nothing without Providence)	Colo.
"Beside the long tidal river"	None	None	Qui transtulit sustinet. (He who transplanted still sustains.)	Conn.
...me of a colonial governor, ...de la Warr	"Our Delaware"	Colonial blue, buff	Liberty and independence	Del.
...: "Flowery"	"Suwannee River"	None	In God we trust.	Fla.
...me of an English king, ...je II	"Georgia"	None	Wisdom, justice, and moderation	Ga.
...wn	"Hawaii Ponoi"	None	Ua Mau Ke Ea O Ka Aina I Ka Pono. (The life of the land is preserved by righteousness.)	None
"The sun is coming down ...ountain"	"Here We Have Idaho"	None	Esto perpetua. (May you last forever.)	None
"Tribe of superior men"	"Illinois"	None	State sovereignty, national union	Ill.
...f Indians	"On the Banks of the Wabash Far Away"	None	The Crossroads of America	Ind.
"This is the place"	"Song of Iowa"	Red, white, blue	Our liberties we prize and our rights we will maintain.	None
"People of the south wind"	"Home on the Range"	None	Ad astra per aspera (To the stars through difficulties)	Kan.
"Land of tomorrow"	"My Old Kentucky Home"	None	United we stand, divided we fall.	Ky.
...me of a French king, ...s XIV	"Song of Louisiana"	None	Union, justice, and confidence	La.
...me of the French ...nce of Mayne	"State of Maine"	None	Dirigo. (I guide.)	Me.
...me of the wife of ...es I of England	"Maryland! My Maryland!"	None	Fatti maschii, parole femine (Manly deeds, womanly words)	Md.
"Big hills"	None	Blue and gold	Ense petit placidam sub libertate quietem. (By the sword we seek peace, but peace only under liberty.)	Mass.
"Great lake"	"Michigan, My Michigan"	None	Si quaeris peninsulam amoenam circumspice. (If you seek a pleasant peninsula, look about you.)	Mich.
"Sky-tinted water"	"Hail Minnesota"	None	L'Etoile du Nord (The North Star)	Minn.
"Father of waters"	"Way Down South in Mississippi"	None	Virtute et armis (By valor and arms)	Miss.

STATE	Year of Admission to Union	Order of Entry	Population (in round numbers)	Area		Capital	Nicknames
				Sq. Mi.	Rank		
MISSOURI	1821	24	4,320,000	69,674	19	Jefferson City	Show-me State
MONTANA	1889	41	675,000	147,138	4	Helena	Treasure State
NEBRASKA	1867	37	1,411,000	77,227	15	Lincoln	Cornhusker State Beef State
NEVADA	1864	36	285,000	110,540	7	Carson City	Sagebrush State Silver State Battle Born State
NEW HAMPSHIRE	1788	9	607,000	9,304	44	Concord	Granite State
NEW JERSEY	1787	3	6,067,000	7,836	46	Trenton	Garden State
NEW MEXICO	1912	47	951,000	121,666	5	Santa Fe	Land of Enchantment Cactus State Sunshine State
NEW YORK	1788	11	16,782,000	49,576	30	Albany	Empire State
NORTH CAROLINA	1789	12	4,556,000	52,712	28	Raleigh	Tarheel State The Old North State
NORTH DAKOTA	1889	39	632,000	70,665	17	Bismarck	Sioux State Flickertail State
OHIO	1803	17	9,706,000	41,222	35	Columbus	Buckeye State
OKLAHOMA	1907	46	2,328,000	69,919	18	Oklahoma City	Sooner State
OREGON	1859	33	1,769,000	96,981	10	Salem	Beaver State
PENNSYLVANIA	1787	2	11,319,000	45,333	33	Harrisburg	Keystone State
RHODE ISLAND	1790	13	859,000	1,214	50	Providence	Little Rhody
SOUTH CAROLINA	1788	8	2,383,000	31,055	40	Columbia	Palmetto State
SOUTH DAKOTA	1889	40	681,000	77,047	16	Pierre	Coyote State Sunshine State
TENNESSEE	1796	16	3,567,000	42,244	34	Nashville	Volunteer State
TEXAS	1845	28	9,580,000	267,339	2	Austin	Lone Star State
UTAH	1896	45	891,000	84,916	11	Salt Lake City	Beehive State
VERMONT	1791	14	390,000	9,609	43	Montpelier	Green Mountain State
VIRGINIA	1788	10	3,967,000	40,815	36	Richmond	The Old Dominion Cavalier State
WASHINGTON	1889	42	2,853,000	68,192	20	Olympia	Evergreen State Chinook State
WEST VIRGINIA	1863	35	1,860,000	24,181	41	Charleston	Mountain State
WISCONSIN	1848	30	3,952,000	56,154	26	Madison	Badger State
WYOMING	1890	44	330,000	97,914	9	Cheyenne	Equality State

Meaning or Origin of Real Name	Songs	Colors	Mottoes	Abbreviation of State Name
n: "People of the big canoes"	"Missouri Waltz"	Red, white, blue	Salus populi suprema lex esto. (The welfare of the people shall be the supreme law.)	Mo.
an: "Mountain land"	"Montana"	None	Oro y plata (Gold and silver)	Mont.
n: "River in the flatness"	"My Nebraska"	None	Equality before the law	Neb.
ish: "Snow-clad"	"Home Means Nevada"	Blue and silver	All for our country	Nev.
name of a county in mpshire	"Old New Hampshire"	None	Live free or die.	N.H.
name of one of the annel Islands, Jersey	None	Blue and buff	Liberty and prosperity	N.J.
the country of Mexico	"O, Fair New Mexico"	Red and orange	Crescit eundo. (It grows as it goes.)	N.M.
itle of an English nobleman, Duke of York	None	None	Excelsior (Ever upward)	N.Y.
ame of an English king, arles I	"The Old North State"	Red and blue	Esse quam videri (To be, rather than to seem)	N.C.
name of an Indian tribe, Dakotas	"North Dakota Hymn"	None	Liberty and union, now and forever: one and inseparable	N.D.
n: "Beautiful river"	None	None	With God, all things are possible.	None
n: "Red people"	"Oklahoma"	Green and white	Labor omnia vincit. (Labor conquers all things.)	Okla.
original name of the umbia River, which meant ace of the beaver"	"Oregon, My Oregon"	Navy, blue, gold	The Union	Ore.
n's Woodland," in honor William Penn's father	None	Blue and gold	Virtue, liberty, and independence	Pa.
name of the Greek island Rhodes	"Rhode Island"	Blue, white, gold	Hope	R.I.
name of an English king, arles I	"Carolina"	None	Animis opibusque parati (Prepared in mind and resources) Dum spiro, spero. (While I breathe, I hope.)	S.C.
name of an Indian tribe, Dakotas	"Hail! South Dakota"	Blue and gold	Under God the people rule.	S.D.
name of an ancient capital the Cherokee Indians	"My Homeland, Tennessee" "When It's Iris Time in Tennessee"	None	Agriculture, commerce	Tenn.
n: "Friends"	"Texas, Our Texas"	None	Friendship	Tex.
name of an Indian tribe, Utes	"Utah, We Love Thee"	None	Industry	None
ch: "Green mountain"	"Hail to Vermont"	None	Freedom and unity	Vt.
Virgin Queen of England, abeth I	"Carry Me Back to Old Virginny"	None	Sic semper tyrannis (Thus always to tyrants)	Va.
name of our first president	"Washington, My Home"	Green and gold	Al-Ki (Bye and bye)	Wash.
Virgin Queen of England, abeth I	"West Virginia Hills" "West Virginia, My Home Sweet Home"	Blue and gold	Montani semper liberi (Mountaineers always free)	W.Va.
n: "Gathering of waters"	"On Wisconsin"	None	Forward	Wis.
n: "Great plains"	"Wyoming"	None	Equal rights	Wyo.

THE PRESIDENTS OF THE UNITED STATES

Name Signature	Time As President	Date of Birth Place of Birth	Date of Death Place of Death	Home S When E
GEORGE WASHINGTON	1789–1797	Feb. 22, 1732 Westmoreland County, Virginia	Dec. 14, 1799 Mount Vernon, Virginia	Virginia
JOHN ADAMS	1797–1801	Oct. 30, 1735 Braintree (later Quincy), Massachusetts	July 4, 1826 Quincy, Massachusetts	Massach
THOMAS JEFFERSON	1801–1809	Apr. 13, 1743 Albemarle County, Virginia	July 4, 1826 Monticello, Virginia	Virginia
JAMES MADISON	1809–1817	Mar. 16, 1751 Port Conway, Virginia	June 28, 1836 Montpelier, Virginia	Virginia
JAMES MONROE	1817–1825	Apr. 28, 1758 Westmoreland County, Virginia	July 4, 1831 New York, New York	Virginia
JOHN QUINCY ADAMS	1825–1829	July 11, 1767 Braintree (later Quincy), Massachusetts	Feb. 23, 1848 Washington, D. C.	Massach
ANDREW JACKSON	1829–1837	Mar. 15, 1767 Lancaster County, South Carolina	June 8, 1845 The Hermitage, Tennessee	Tenness

Political Party	Occupation	Religion	Name of Wife Number of Children	Important Events during Term in Office
...ty ...irst ...d. ...d term: ...list	Plantation owner, Soldier, Surveyor	Episcopalian	Martha Dandridge Custis No children	First census taken. Cotton gin invented. Whiskey Rebellion put down. New capital planned. Bank of the United States established.
...list	Lawyer, Legislator, Diplomat	Unitarian	Abigail Smith 3 sons, 2 daughters	XYZ Affair settled. Washington, D.C., made the capital. Alien and Sedition Acts passed. Navy Department created. White House made the official home of president.
...cratic- ...lican	Lawyer, Diplomat, Legislator, Architect, Writer	Deist	Martha Wayles Skelton 1 son, 5 daughters	Louisiana Territory purchased from France. Steamboat invented. West Point established. War fought with Barbary pirates. Lewis and Clark expedition.
...cratic- ...lican	Plantation owner, Legislator, Writer	Episcopalian	Dorothy ("Dolley") Payne Todd No children	War of 1812. Washington burned by the British. British ship "Guerriere" sunk by "Old Ironsides." "The Star Spangled Banner" written. Cumberland Road begun.
...cratic- ...lican	Lawyer, Soldier, Legislator, Diplomat	Episcopalian	Eliza Kortright 2 daughters	Monroe Doctrine proclaimed. Florida purchased from Spain. First public high school opened. Canadian-United States boundary established. The Atlantic first crossed by steamship.
...cratic- ...lican	Lawyer, Diplomat, Legislator,	Unitarian	Louisa Catherine Johnson 3 sons, 1 daughter	Erie Canal opened. First passenger railroad built. Bunker Hill Monument built. Webster's Dictionary published. First Pan-American conference held.
...cratic	Lawyer, Soldier	Presbyterian	Rachel Donelson Robards No children	Reaper invented by McCormick. Friction match first patented in America. Postmaster General added to Cabinet. Independence won by Texas from Mexico. Black Hawk War.

THE PRESIDENTS OF THE UNITED STATES

Name Signature	Time As President	Date of Birth Place of Birth	Date of Death Place of Death	Home When
★★★★★★★★★ MARTIN VAN BUREN *m van Buren*	1837– 1841	Dec. 5, 1782 Kinderhook, New York	July 24, 1862 Kinderhook, New York	New Y
★★★★★★★★★ WILLIAM HENRY HARRISON *W H Harrison*	1841 (1 month)	Feb. 9, 1773 Charles City County, Virginia	April 4, 1841 Washington, D. C.	Ohio
★★★★★★★★★ JOHN TYLER *John Tyler*	1841– 1845	Mar. 29, 1790 Charles City County, Virginia	Jan. 18, 1862 Sherwood Forest, Virginia	Virgini
★★★★★★★★★ JAMES K. POLK *James K Polk*	1845– 1849	Nov. 2, 1795 Mecklenburg County, North Carolina	June 15, 1849 Nashville, Tennessee	Tennes
★★★★★★★★★ ZACHARY TAYLOR *Zachary Taylor*	1849– 1850	Nov. 24, 1784 Orange County, Virginia	July 9, 1850 Washington, D. C.	Louisia
★★★★★★★★★ MILLARD FILLMORE *Millard Fillmore*	1850– 1853	Jan. 7, 1800 Cayuga County, New York	Mar. 8, 1874 Buffalo, New York	New Yc
★★★★★★★★★ FRANKLIN PIERCE *Franklin Pierce*	1853– 1857	Nov. 23, 1804 Hillsboro, New Hampshire	Oct. 8, 1869 Concord, New Hampshire	New Ha

ical	Occupation	Religion	Name of Wife Number of Children	Important Events during Term in Office
ratic	Lawyer, Legislator	Reformed Dutch	Hannah Hoes 4 sons	Telegraph invented by Morse. Vulcanization of rubber discovered by Goodyear. First photograph taken in the United States. War with Seminole Indians waged. Aroostook War between Maine and New Brunswick.
	Soldier, Territorial governor	Episcopalian	Anna Symmes 6 sons, 4 daughters	(First president to die in office.) Daniel Webster appointed Secretary of State.
	Lawyer, Legislator	Episcopalian	Letitia Christian 3 sons, 4 daughters Julia Gardiner 5 sons, 2 daughters	First telegraph line built. Seminole War ended. Ashburton Treaty with Britain signed. Emigrants surged westward over the Oregon Trail. Door opened by treaty to trade with China.
ratic	Lawyer, Legislator	Methodist	Sarah Childress No children	Gold discovered in California. Mexican War. Sewing machine invented. Utah settled by Mormons. U.S. Naval Academy established at Annapolis.
	Soldier	Episcopalian	Margaret Mackall Smith 1 son, 5 daughters	Gold rush to California. First step toward Panama Canal taken. Department of Interior established. Treaty with Hawaii signed. Many debates about slavery held.
	Lawyer, Legislator	Episcopalian	Abigail Powers 1 son, 1 daughter Caroline McIntosh No children	"Uncle Tom's Cabin" published. First American concert by Jenny Lind given. Clay compromise agreed upon. "Old Folks at Home" by Stephen Foster published. Record for clipper ships set by "Flying Cloud."
ratic	Lawyer, Legislator, Soldier	Episcopalian	Jane Means Appleton 3 sons	Japan opened to trade as a result of visits of Commodore Perry. Republican Party formed. First railroad built across Mississippi River. Kansas-Nebraska Act passed.

THE PRESIDENTS OF THE UNITED STATES

Name Signature	Time As President	Date of Birth Place of Birth	Date of Death Place of Death	Home When
JAMES BUCHANAN	1857– 1861	Apr. 23, 1791 near Mercersburg, Pennsylvania	June 1, 1868 near Lancaster, Pennsylvania	Penn
ABRAHAM LINCOLN	1861– 1865	Feb. 12, 1809 Hardin County (now Larue), Kentucky	Apr. 15, 1865 Washington, D. C.	Illinoi
ANDREW JOHNSON	1865– 1869	Dec. 29, 1808 Raleigh, North Carolina	July 31, 1875 near Carter Station, Tennessee	Tenn
ULYSSES S. GRANT	1869– 1877	Apr. 27, 1822 Point Pleasant, Ohio	July 23, 1885 Mount McGregor, New York	Illinoi
RUTHERFORD B. HAYES	1877– 1881	Oct. 4, 1822 Delaware, Ohio	Jan. 17, 1893 Fremont, Ohio	Ohio
JAMES A. GARFIELD	Mar.– Sept., 1881	Nov. 19, 1831 Cuyahoga County, Ohio	Sept. 19, 1881 Elberon, New Jersey	Ohio
CHESTER A. ARTHUR	1881– 1885	Oct. 5, 1830 Fairfield, Vermont	Nov. 18, 1886 New York, New York	New Y

cal	Occupation	Religion	Name of Wife Number of Children	Important Events during Term in Office
ratic	Lawyer, Legislator, Diplomat	Presbyterian	None	First cable laid across Atlantic. Lincoln-Douglas debates held. Pony Express established. First oil well drilled. Confederate States organized.
ican	Lawyer, Legislator	Liberal	Mary Todd 4 sons	Emancipation Proclamation freed slaves of South. War between the States. Free mail delivery established in cities. Department of Agriculture established. Transcontinental telegraph line completed.
	Tailor, Legislator	Methodist	Eliza McCardle 3 sons, 2 daughters	Alaska purchased. Typewriter invented. First refrigerator car built. First plastics made. Bureau of Education established.
ican	Soldier	Methodist	Julia Dent 3 sons, 1 daughter	Centennial Exposition in Philadelphia. Telephone invented. First national park established. First transcontinental railroad completed. National Baseball League formed. Chicago fire.
ican	Lawyer, Soldier	Methodist	Lucy Ware Webb 7 sons, 1 daughter	Phonograph invented. Electric light bulb invented. Salvation Army organized in the United States. First 5 and 10 cent stores established. Federal troops withdrawn from South.
ican	College president, Soldier, Legislator	Disciples of Christ	Lucretia Rudolph 5 sons, 2 daughters	American Red Cross organized. Tuskegee Institute established.
ican	Lawyer	Episcopalian	Ellen Lewis Herndon 2 sons, 1 daughter	First skyscraper built. Brooklyn Bridge completed. Washington Monument dedicated. American Federation of Labor formed. Standard time adopted.

THE PRESIDENTS OF THE UNITED STATES

Name Signature	Time As President	Date of Birth Place of Birth	Date of Death Place of Death	Home Wher
GROVER CLEVELAND	1885–1889 1893–1897	Mar. 18, 1837 Caldwell, New Jersey	June 24, 1908 Princeton, New Jersey	New
BENJAMIN HARRISON	1889– 1893	Aug. 20, 1833 North Bend, Ohio	Mar. 13, 1901 Indianapolis, Indiana	Indi
WILLIAM McKINLEY	1897– 1901	Jan. 29, 1843 Niles, Ohio	Sept. 14, 1901 Buffalo, New York	Ohio
THEODORE ROOSEVELT	1901– 1909	Oct. 27, 1858 New York, New York	Jan. 6, 1919 Oyster Bay, New York	New
WILLIAM HOWARD TAFT	1909– 1913	Sept. 15, 1857 Cincinnati, Ohio	Mar. 8, 1930 Washington, D. C.	Ohio
WOODROW WILSON	1913– 1921	Dec. 28, 1856 Staunton, Virginia	Feb. 3, 1924 Washington, D. C.	New
WARREN G. HARDING	1921– 1923	Nov. 2, 1865 Morrow County, Ohio	Aug. 2, 1923 San Francisco, California	Ohio

al	Occupation	Religion	Name of Wife Number of Children	Important Events during Term in Office
ratic	Lawyer	Presbyterian	Frances Folsom 2 sons, 3 daughters	Statue of Liberty dedicated. United States given right to enter Pearl Harbor. Secretary of Agriculture added to Cabinet. Columbian Exposition in Chicago. Ford's first car appeared.
can	Lawyer	Presbyterian	Caroline Scott 1 son, 1 daughter Mary Scott Dimmock 1 daughter	First Carnegie library opened. Four American battleships built. Oklahoma opened to homesteaders. International Copyright Act passed. Six northwest states added to Union.
can	Soldier, Lawyer	Methodist	Ida Saxton 2 daughters	Alaskan gold rush. Spanish-American War. Yellow fever conquered. Policy of open door in China accepted. American Baseball League formed.
can	Soldier, Government official	Reformed Dutch	Alice Hathaway Lee 1 daughter Edith Kermit Carow 4 sons, 1 daughter	Department of Commerce and Labor established. Wright brothers' airplane flight. U.S. Forest Service created. Pacific cable laid and wireless service across Atlantic begun. San Francisco earthquake.
can	Lawyer, Diplomat	Unitarian	Helen Herron 2 sons, 1 daughter	North Pole reached by Peary. South Pole reached by Amundsen. Parcel post service begun. Roosevelt Dam completed. Boy Scouts of America organized.
ratic	Teacher, Lawyer, College president	Presbyterian	Ellen Louise Axson 3 daughters Edith Bolling Galt No children	World War I. Panama Canal opened. First air mail route set up. League of Nations established. Women given right to vote. First radio program broadcast.
can	Newspaper editor and publisher	Baptist	Florence Kling De Wolfe No children	Lincoln Memorial dedicated. Peace Treaty with Germany signed. Unknown Soldier buried at Arlington. New quota plan of immigration set up.

THE PRESIDENTS OF THE UNITED STATES

Name Signature	Time As President	Date of Birth Place of Birth	Date of Death Place of Death	Home When
CALVIN COOLIDGE	1923–1929	July 4, 1872 Plymouth, Vermont	Jan. 5, 1933 Northampton, Massachusetts	Massa
HERBERT HOOVER	1929–1933	Aug. 10, 1874 West Branch, Iowa		Califo
FRANKLIN D. ROOSEVELT	1933–1945	Jan. 30, 1882 Hyde Park, New York	April 12, 1945 Warm Springs, Georgia	New Y
HARRY S. TRUMAN	1945–1953	May 8, 1884 Lamar, Missouri		Misso
DWIGHT D. EISENHOWER	1953–1961	Oct. 14, 1890 Denison, Texas		New Y
JOHN F. KENNEDY	1961–	May 29, 1917 Brookline, Massachusetts		Massa

QUALIFICATIONS

To be eligible for the office of President of the United States, a person must be a natural-born citizen of the country, must be 35 years old, and must have lived in the country for at least 14 years.

PRESIDENTIAL OATH

"I do solemnly swear (or affirm) that I will faithfully execute the Office of President of the United States, and will, to the best of my ability, preserve, protect, and defend the Constitution of the United States."

itical ty	Occupation	Religion	Name of Wife Number of Children	Important Events during Term in Office
blican	Lawyer	Congregationalist	Grace Anna Goodhue 2 sons	Atlantic crossed by Lindbergh in solo flight. First trip around the world by air made. Flight across North Pole made by Byrd. Soldiers' Bonus Bill passed. Talking movies introduced.
blican	Mining engineer, Business executive	Quaker	Lou Henry 2 sons	Stock market crash and great depression. Veterans Administration established. "Old Ironsides" rebuilt. Manchuria invaded by Japan. In Germany Hitler made chancellor
cratic	Lawyer, Government official	Episcopalian	Anna Eleanor Roosevelt 5 sons, 1 daughter	World War II. Radar invented. CIO (Congress of Industrial Organizations) formed. First controlled nuclear chain reaction. Social Security Act passed.
cratic	Businessman, Judge, Legislator	Baptist	Bess Wallace 1 daughter	World War II brought to an end. United Nations established. Korean War. Philippines made an independent republic. NATO (North Atlantic Treaty Organization) created.
blican	Soldier, College president	Presbyterian	Mamie Geneva Doud 2 sons	Alaska and Hawaii added as new states. Polio vaccine developed. First atomic power station and submarine built. Jet airplane passenger service established. First satellites launched.
cratic	Legislator, Author	Roman Catholic	Jacqueline Lee Bouvier 1 son, 1 daughter	First spacemen circle earth. Peace Corps established. Alliance for Progress formed. First nuclear-powered aircraft carrier built.

PRESIDENTIAL SUCCESSION

In the event of the death or disability of the President of the United States, the Vice-President becomes President. In case he dies or is disabled, the Speaker of the House succeeds him. Next in order of succession comes the President of the Senate. The Cabinet officers then follow in this order: Secretary of State, Secretary of the Treasury, Secretary of Defense, Attorney General, Postmaster General, Secretary of the Interior, Secretary of Agriculture, Secretary of Commerce, Secretary of Labor, and Secretary of Health, Education, and Welfare.

CLASSIFICATION OF LIVING THINGS

In classifying plants and animals, scientists group the plants and animals that are very much alike into species. Species that are much alike are grouped into genera (the plural of genus). Genera are put together to form families, families make up orders, orders make up classes, and classes make up phyla. For an even more exact classification, classes may be grouped into subphyla and the subphyla into phyla. There may also be suborders, subgenera, and so on. Subspecies are often called varieties.

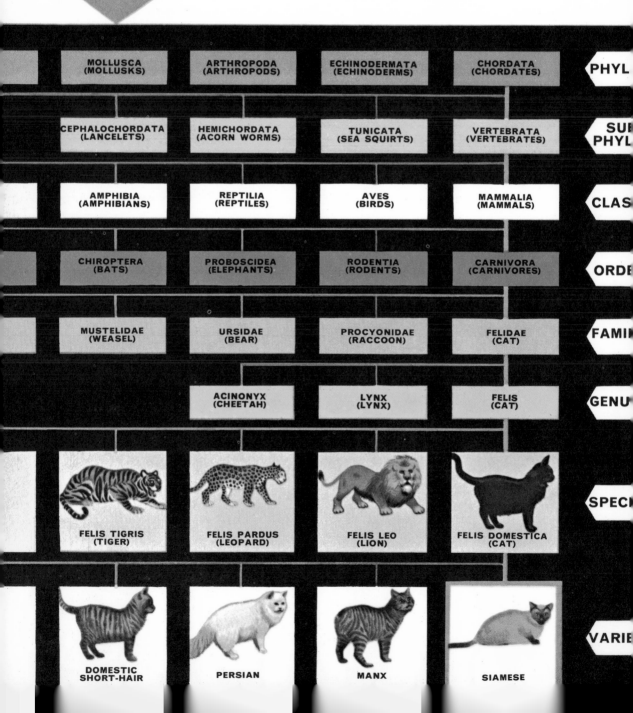

MOLLUSCA (MOLLUSKS)	ARTHROPODA (ARTHROPODS)	ECHINODERMATA (ECHINODERMS)	CHORDATA (CHORDATES)	**PHYL**
CEPHALOCHORDATA (LANCELETS)	HEMICHORDATA (ACORN WORMS)	TUNICATA (SEA SQUIRTS)	VERTEBRATA (VERTEBRATES)	**SUB PHYL**
AMPHIBIA (AMPHIBIANS)	REPTILIA (REPTILES)	AVES (BIRDS)	MAMMALIA (MAMMALS)	**CLAS**
CHIROPTERA (BATS)	PROBOSCIDEA (ELEPHANTS)	RODENTIA (RODENTS)	CARNIVORA (CARNIVORES)	**ORDE**
MUSTELIDAE (WEASEL)	URSIDAE (BEAR)	PROCYONIDAE (RACCOON)	FELIDAE (CAT)	**FAMI**
	ACINONYX (CHEETAH)	LYNX (LYNX)	FELIS (CAT)	**GENU**
FELIS TIGRIS (TIGER)	FELIS PARDUS (LEOPARD)	FELIS LEO (LION)	FELIS DOMESTICA (CAT)	**SPECI**
DOMESTIC SHORT-HAIR	PERSIAN	MANX	SIAMESE	**VARIE**

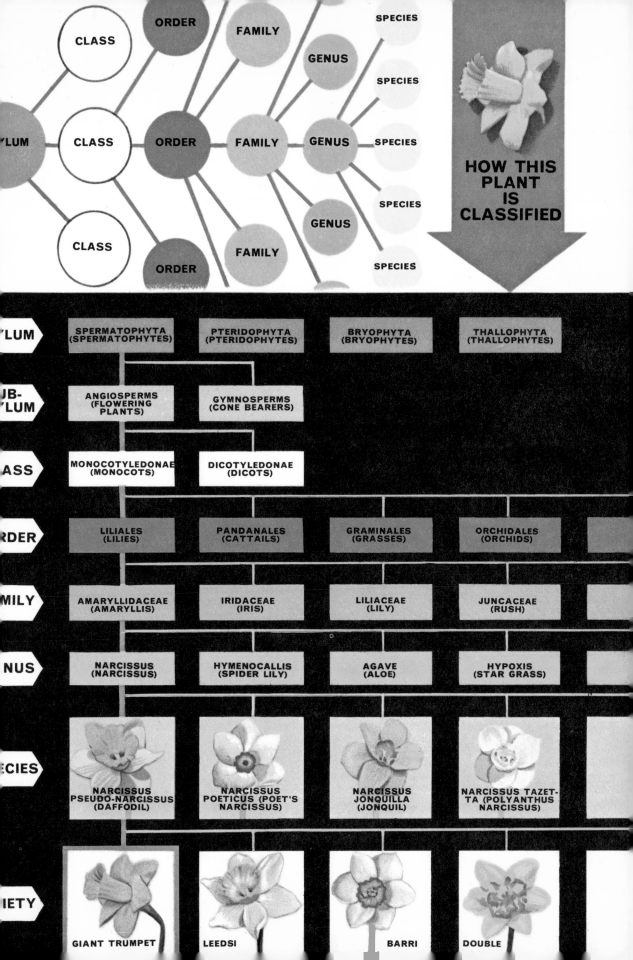

CLASS ORDER FAMILY SPECIES

GENUS SPECIES

PHYLUM CLASS ORDER FAMILY GENUS SPECIES

CLASS GENUS SPECIES

FAMILY

CLASS ORDER SPECIES

HOW THIS PLANT IS CLASSIFIED

| PHYLUM | SPERMATOPHYTA (SPERMATOPHYTES) | PTERIDOPHYTA (PTERIDOPHYTES) | BRYOPHYTA (BRYOPHYTES) | THALLOPHYTA (THALLOPHYTES) |

| SUB-PHYLUM | ANGIOSPERMS (FLOWERING PLANTS) | GYMNOSPERMS (CONE BEARERS) |

| CLASS | MONOCOTYLEDONAE (MONOCOTS) | DICOTYLEDONAE (DICOTS) |

| ORDER | LILIALES (LILIES) | PANDANALES (CATTAILS) | GRAMINALES (GRASSES) | ORCHIDALES (ORCHIDS) |

| FAMILY | AMARYLLIDACEAE (AMARYLLIS) | IRIDACEAE (IRIS) | LILIACEAE (LILY) | JUNCACEAE (RUSH) |

| GENUS | NARCISSUS (NARCISSUS) | HYMENOCALLIS (SPIDER LILY) | AGAVE (ALOE) | HYPOXIS (STAR GRASS) |

| SPECIES | NARCISSUS PSEUDO-NARCISSUS (DAFFODIL) | NARCISSUS POETICUS (POET'S NARCISSUS) | NARCISSUS JONQUILLA (JONQUIL) | NARCISSUS TAZETTA (POLYANTHUS NARCISSUS) |

| VARIETY | GIANT TRUMPET | LEEDSI | BARRI | DOUBLE |

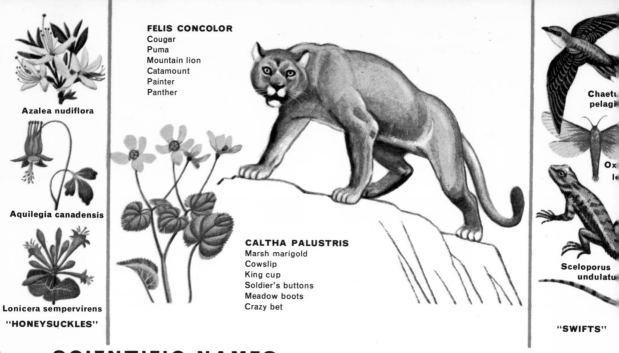

FELIS CONCOLOR
Cougar
Puma
Mountain lion
Catamount
Painter
Panther

Azalea nudiflora

Aquilegia canadensis

Lonicera sempervirens
"HONEYSUCKLES"

CALTHA PALUSTRIS
Marsh marigold
Cowslip
King cup
Soldier's buttons
Meadow boots
Crazy bet

Chaetu
pelagi

Ox
le

Sceloporus
undulatu

"SWIFTS"

SCIENTIFIC NAMES

One kind of plant or animal may have several common names in our language. The yellow-hammer, high-hole, flicker, and golden-winged woodpecker, for instance, are all the same bird. If the plant or animal is found in other countries, it is almost sure to have common names in other languages. Several different kinds of plants or animals, moreover, may have the same common name. At least a dozen kinds of plants are called bluebells. Common names, therefore, may be confusing. To avoid confusion scientists have given all plants and animals scientific names.

Scientific names are in Latin and are used by scientists all over the world. The scientific name of a plant or animal is almost always made up of at least two words. The first tells the genus. The second tells the species. If a plant or animal belongs to a subspecies, a third word in its name tells its subspecies. The list below gives the scientific names of some well-known plants and animals.

COMMON NAME	SCIENTIFIC NAME
Alligator, American	**Alligator mississippiensis**
Ant, little black	**Monomorium minimum**
Apple	**Pyrus malus**
Ash, white	**Fraxinus americana**
Banana	**Musa paradisiaca sapientum**
Barley	**Hordeum vulgare**
Bear, grizzly	**Ursus horribilis**
Bison, American	**Bison bison**
Blackbird, yellow-headed	**Xanthocephalus xanthocephalus**
Bluebird	**Sialia sialis**
Bluegrass, Kentucky	**Poa pratensis**
Blueberry, high-bush	**Vaccinium corymbosum**
Blue jay	**Cyanocitta cristata**
Blue whale	**Sibbaldus musculus**
Bobwhite	**Colinus virginianus**
Bridalwreath	**Spiraea prunifolia**
Bullfrog	**Rana catesbeiana**
Cabbage	**Brassica oleracea capitata**
Camel, Arabian	**Camelus dromedarius**
Carnation	**Dianthus caryophyllus**
Carrot	**Daucus carota sativa**
Cat	**Felis domestica**
Cecropia moth	**Platysamia cecropia**
Chicken	**Gallus domesticus**
Chimpanzee	**Pan**, or **Anthropopithecus troglodytes**

COMMON NAME	SCIENTIFIC NAME
Clover, red	**Trifolium pratense**
Coconut	**Cocos nucifera**
Corn	**Zea mays**
Cotton	**Gossypium hirsutum**
Cow	**Bos taurus**
Cranberry	**Vaccinium oxycoccos**
Dandelion, common	**Taraxacum officinale**
Dog	**Canis familiaris**
Donkey	**Equus asinus**
Duck, mallard	**Anas platyrhynchos**
Earthworm	**Lumbricus terrestris**
Eel, common	**Anguilla rostrata**
Elephant, African	**Loxodonta africana**
Elm, American	**Ulmus americana**
English or House sparrow	**Passer domesticus**
Flax	**Linum usitatissimum**
Fly (housefly)	**Musca domestica**
Garden spider, golden	**Argiope aurantia**
Garter snake	**Thamnophis ordinatus**
Geranium	**Pelargonium hortorum**
Giraffe	**Giraffa camelopardalis**
Goat, Angora	**Capra angorensis**
Goldenrod, Canadian	**Solidago canadensis**
Goldfish	**Carassius auratus**
Gorilla	**Gorilla gorilla**
Grapefruit	**Citrus paradisi**
Hippopotamus	**Hippopotamus amphibius**

Taraxacum officinale

Pinus strobus

Acer saccharum

Zea mays

Tulipa gesneriana

COMMON NAME	SCIENTIFIC NAME	COMMON NAME	SCIENTIFIC NAME
Honeybee	**Apis mellifera**	Pussy willow	**Salix discolor**
Horse	**Equus caballus**	Radish	**Raphanus sativus**
Hummingbird, ruby-throated	**Archilochus colubris**	Ragweed, giant	**Ambrosia trifida**
Lemon	**Citrus limonia**	Raspberry, red	**Rubus idaeus strigosus**
Lettuce	**Lactuca sativa**	Rat, Norway	**Rattus norvegicus**
Lily, Easter	**Lilium candidum**	Reindeer, American	**Rangifer arcticus**
Lima bean	**Phaseolus limensis**	Rhinoceros	**Diceros bicornis**
Lobster	**Homarus americanus**	Robin	**Turdus migratorius**
Man	**Homo sapiens**	Rose, meadow (wild)	**Rosa blanda**
Maple, sugar	**Acer saccharum**	Rye	**Secale cereale**
Marigold, French	**Tagetes patula**	Saguaro	**Carnegiea gigantea**
Mosquito, house	**Culex pipiens**	Salmon, Chinook	**Oncorhynchus tshawytscha**
Mouse, house	**Mus musculus**	Scallop, bay	**Aequipecten irradians**
Nasturtium	**Tropaeolum majus**	Sea horse	**Hippocampus hudsonius**
Oak, black	**Quercus velutina**	Sheep	**Ovis aries**
Oak, white	**Quercus alba**	Silkworm	**Bombyx mori**
Oats	**Avena sativa**	Soybean	**Glycine max**
Onion	**Allium cepa**	Squash, summer	**Cucurbita pepo condensa**
Orange	**Citrus sinensis**	Squirrel, gray	**Sciurus carolinensis**
Ostrich, South African	**Struthio australis**	Starfish, common	**Asterias forbesi**
Oyster	**Crassostrea virginica**	Strawberry	**Fragaria chiloensis**
Painted turtle	**Chrysemys picta marginata**	Sunflower	**Helianthus decapetalus**
Pea, garden	**Pisum sativum**	Swallowtail, black	**Papilio polyxenes asterias**
Peach	**Prunus persica**	Thistle, Canada	**Cirsium arvense**
Peacock	**Pavo cristatus**	Toad, common	**Bufo americanus**
Pear	**Pyrus communis**	Tobacco	**Nicotiana tabacum**
Petunia	**Petunia hybrida**	Tree-of-heaven	**Ailanthus altissima**
Pig	**Sus scrofa**	Tulip	**Tulipa gesneriana**
Pine, white	**Pinus strobus**	Turkey	**Meleagris gallopavo**
Poison ivy	**Rhus toxicodendron**	Violet, African	**Saintpaulia ionantha**
Portuguese man-of-war	**Physalia physalis**	Violet, common blue	**Viola cucullata**
Potato	**Solanum tuberosum**	Walnut, black	**Juglans nigra**
Praying mantis	**Paratenodera sinensis**	Wheat	**Triticum sativum**
Pumpkin	**Cucurbita pepo**	Zebra	**Equus burchelli**

Cyanocitta cristata

Papilio polyxenes asterias

Equus caballus

Canis familiaris

FOOD PYRAMIDS

Lions eat zebras. Zebras eat grass. Thus the lion, the zebra, and grass make a food chain. It takes a great deal of grass to feed one zebra for a year, and it takes about 50 zebras to feed a lion for a year. This story can be told by a diagram called a food pyramid. The chart at the right shows several food pyramids.

Notice that green plants form the base of each one of these pyramids. The food of every animal can be traced back to green plants. At the top of most pyramids there is a meat-eating animal.

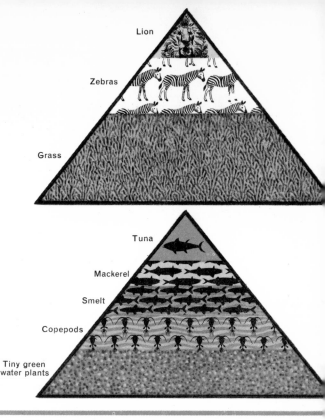

Lion

Zebras

Grass

Tuna

Mackerel

Smelt

Copepods

Tiny green
water plants

LIVING FOSSILS

Some kinds of plants and animals have lived on, almost unchanged, for millions of years after most or all of their close relatives became extinct. These plants and animals are often called living fossils.

LINGULA
Lingula is one of the group of little-known marine animals called brachiopods. It has remained almost exactly the same for about half a billion years. It dates back to the time when there were no animals anywhere with backbones, and when brachiopods were very common and ranked high among the animals of the earth. No other genus of animals has so long a history.

GINKGO TREE
The famous scientist Darwin called attention to this tree as a "living fossil." It is the only plant left of a group that flourished in the days of the dinosaurs. The ginkgo is a seed plant, but it is of a primitive kind. Once spread far and wide over the earth, this tree is now found growing wild only in a few places in China.

COELACANTH
The fish in the picture is sometimes called a "fossil come to life." Until 1939 scientists thought that all the coelacanths had disappeared about 70 million years ago. But in 1939 a coelacanth was dredged up by a fishing trawler near the tip of South Africa. Since then several other specimens have been found. The coelacanth is a lobefin. It is almost exactly like its ancestors that lived in the last days of the dinosaurs.

PERIPATUS
This worm does not have any common name, not because it is a newcomer on the earth, but because few people ever see it. It is very much like its ancestors that left their traces in rocks formed 500 million years ago. It has been called the "worm that didn't turn—into anything." Peripatus has never been found north of the tropics.

AUSTRALIAN LUNGFISH
The Australian lungfish is another fossil come to life. For a long time it was known only through its fossils, some of which were found in rocks 200 million years old. But in 1869 living specimens were found.

HORSESHOE CRAB
The horseshoe crab is not a true crab. It has no very close relatives in the world today. For 200 million years it has been able to hold its own with practically no change.

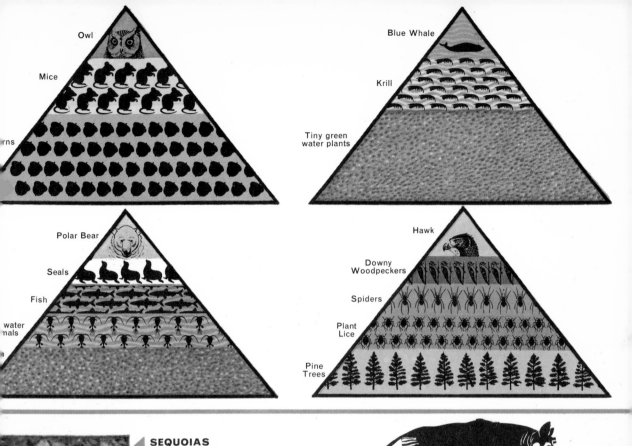

SEQUOIAS

The first sequoia-like trees appeared more than 100 million years ago, during the Age of Reptiles. They were very successful. In time there were many species of sequoias, probably more than a hundred, and they formed great forests in Europe and Asia as well as in the Americas. They were the lords of the plant world. But now only two kinds of sequoias are left—the big tree and the coast redwood—and they are found only in small areas near the western coast of the United States. The metasequoia, a closely related tree, is another fossil come to life. It was long believed to be extinct but was recently discovered in central China. Its common name is dawn redwood.

OKAPI

The okapi deserves the name of "living fossil" because it is almost exactly like its ancestors of 30 million years ago. It has no close relatives. Its closest relative is the giraffe.

TUATARA

This small reptile has remained almost unchanged for more than 200 million years. During its long history on the earth its relatives the dinosaurs, pterosaurs, ichthyosaurs, and plesiosaurs appeared, became the earth's leading animals, and then completely died out. Today the tuatara is found only on some small islands near New Zealand.

WELWITSCHIA

This queer plant is another holdover from nature's early experiments with seed plants. It is quite unlike any other plant in the world. There are only two other plants that are at all closely related, and they do not look like welwitschia. This holdover from long ago grows only in southwestern Africa.

page 83

Franklinia This beautiful tree was named for Benjamin Franklin. A friend of his found it growing in the woods of southeastern Georgia, and brought some specimens home to Philadelphia. All the Franklinia trees we know of now are descendants of these trees that were brought to Philadelphia. For since 1790, twenty-five years after it was discovered, no one has been able to find it growing wild.

Torrey pine This is America's rarest pine. It grows wild only on a narrow strip of land in southern California and on the island of Santa Rosa. It is planted in New Zealand and in some California parks.

Showy lady's-slipper This orchid is one of the most beautiful of our wild flowers. Too much picking has put it in danger of disappearing.

Trailing arbutus Careless picking has also reduced the numbers of this beautiful little plant. It is protected by law in some states, but there is still danger that it will not survive.

Monterey cypress This tree grows wild in only two very small areas in California. There little by little the cliffs where it grows are crumbling away. But the tree has a chance of living since it is being cultivated in several parts of the world.

Port Orford cedar This rare cedar has been called the most beautiful of the large conifers. It grows only in a narrow strip in the mountains of California and Oregon. The wood of this tree is much wanted by builders. Many trees have been cut for matchsticks!

FOSSILS OF THE FUTURE

Many, many of the plants and animals of long ago have become extinct. We know about them only through fossils, traces in the rocks of the living things of the past. Some present-day plants and animals are in danger of disappearing. In time only fossils of them may be left. These are a few of the living things that, unless great care is taken, are likely to be merely fossils in the not-too-distant future.

Solenodon This small insect eater was once found in both Cuba and Hispaniola. It is now believed to have disappeared from Cuba and is in danger of disappearing from Hispaniola, too. Its chief enemy has been the mongoose, which was brought to the West Indies to control rats. It found the solenodon easier to catch.

Tasmanian wolf This animal is perhaps the rarest mammal in the world. The only ones remaining are in the mountains of Tasmania. The Tasmanian wolf is not a true wolf. It is a pouched mammal, or marsupial, and is therefore a closer relative of the kangaroo than of the wolf. At times, in fact, it hops on its hind legs like a kangaroo. But, like the true wolves, it is a meat-eater.

Sea otter At one time the pelt of a sea otter brought as much as $2,500.00. So many otters were killed for their fur that for years scientists thought the animal was extinct. But then a small herd was found and a protecting law was passed. There is some hope that the otter may be saved.

One-horned rhinoceros of Java Only about 40 Javanese rhinos are left. These are all on a government preserve in western Java. For centuries the natives of Java and the region round about have believed that the powdered horn and skin of the rhinoceros made good medicine for diseases of many kinds. The Indian rhinoceros is also in danger. It has been almost killed off for the same reason. As much as $2,500.00 has been paid for a single rhinoceros horn.

...ing crane So far as ...knows, there are only ...wild whooping cranes ...air of cranes, crippled ...they cannot fly, live in a ...New Orleans. Scientists ...at young birds hatched ...eir eggs will help keep ...d from disappearing.

Ivory-billed woodpecker Probably the ivory-billed woodpecker has completely disappeared in the United States. But there are still at least a few left in Cuba. They are so scarce, however, that it is hard to believe that they will survive.

Teita falcon of Africa This bird has been found only eight times in the past 65 years. It would seem that there was not much chance of its surviving, but it may be holding its own in some of the little-known parts of Africa.

California condor This bird of prey is the world's largest flying land bird. Only about 60 are left. They now live in a refuge where they are safe from hunters.

...lion This lion was once common in many parts of Asia. Now not more than ...eft. They are in a forest in northwestern India, where they are protected. The ... the lion was a danger to cattle, camels, and horses made the natives kill it ...er they could. Besides, Indian maharajahs for years considered lion-hunting ...g sport.

Oryx of Arabia This oryx is one of the many antelopes of the Old World. To an Arab, killing an oryx is something to boast about, for it is very fast. The only ones left are now in the almost empty desert Rub 'al Khali in southern Arabia. Less than 100 are left. Even these will soon be gone if the Arabian princes keep on hunting them from automobiles and airplanes.

Giant sable antelope of Africa A few hundred of these big antelopes are left on a government preserve in Portuguese Angola. But even some of those are being killed by poachers, who know that the long curved horns will bring a high price.

Brow-antlered deer of Burma The once vast herds of this deer have been almost wiped out, partly because many have been killed for food and partly because people have settled the marshy region where they live. Now the natives believe that eating the meat of this deer causes disease and the killing has stopped. But it is probably too late to save the deer since there are only about 200 left.

European bison, or wisent Refuges were set up for the American bison before it was too late. Although refuges have now been set up for the European bison, less than 100 are left and the chances of saving this big animal are not good.

Banded anteater of Australia This anteater is, like the Tasmanian wolf, a pouched mammal. Not people but wild dogs are chiefly to blame for the scarcity of this animal.

page 85

FLOWER PARTS

Complete flowers have parts of four kinds. These parts are called pistils, stamens, petals, and sepals.

The pistils contain ovules which, when fertilized by means of pollen, become seeds. The part of a pistil containing the ovules is the *ovary*. Above the ovary is the *style*. The style has at some place, usually its top, a sticky surface called a *stigma*. The stigma serves to hold in place the pollen that reaches it.

Each stamen ends in an *anther*, or pollen sac, in which pollen is formed. The stalk of a stamen is its *filament*.

The petals surround the stamens and pistils. As a rule they form the showy part of the flower. The petals together make up the *corolla*.

The sepals are outside the petals and in many cases form a protective covering when the flower is in bud. The sepals together make up the *calyx*.

Pollen
Anther

Stigma

Style

Petal

Filament

Ovule

Ovary

Sepal

Receptacle

TRILLIUM

STAMEN   PISTIL

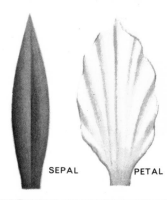

SEPAL   PETAL

FLOWER PATTERN

PISTIL   PETAL

STAMEN   SEPAL

TYPES OF FLOWERS

TULIP AND IRIS
In some flowers, such as the tulip and the iris, the sepals are as showy as the petals. They can be told from the petals because they are outside the petals.

STAMINATE FLOWER   PISTILLATE FLOWER

WILLOW
Willows have two kinds of flowers. One kind has a pistil but no stamens; the other stamens but no pistil. In most cases the two kinds are on different plants. Most willows are therefore said to be dioecious (two households). Willow flowers have no petals or sepals; each flower is protected by a little leaf called a bract.

MORNING-GLORY
In the morning-glory the petals are joined together. Such flowers are sympetalous.

POINSETTIA
What appears to be a big flower on a poinsettia plant is really a group of small flowers surrounded by a circle of showy colored leaves.

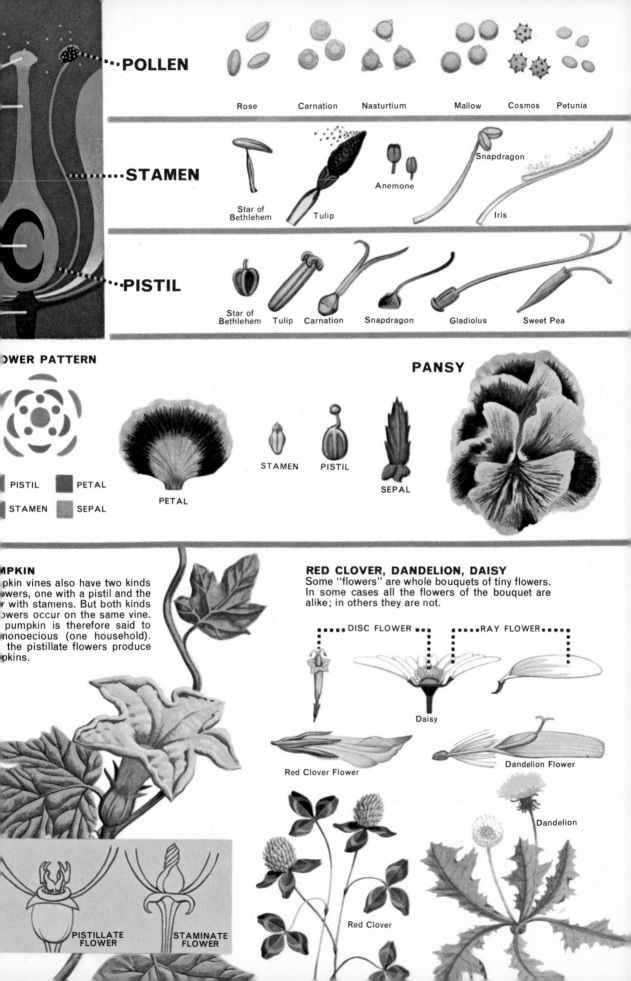

POLLEN

Rose · Carnation · Nasturtium · Mallow · Cosmos · Petunia

STAMEN

Star of Bethlehem · Tulip · Anemone · Snapdragon · Iris

PISTIL

Star of Bethlehem · Tulip · Carnation · Snapdragon · Gladiolus · Sweet Pea

FLOWER PATTERN

PISTIL · PETAL
STAMEN · SEPAL

PETAL · STAMEN · PISTIL · SEPAL

PANSY

PUMPKIN

...pkin vines also have two kinds
...owers, one with a pistil and the
... with stamens. But both kinds
...owers occur on the same vine.
... pumpkin is therefore said to
...nonoecious (one household).
... the pistillate flowers produce
...pkins.

PISTILLATE FLOWER · STAMINATE FLOWER

RED CLOVER, DANDELION, DAISY

Some "flowers" are whole bouquets of tiny flowers.
In some cases all the flowers of the bouquet are
alike; in others they are not.

DISC FLOWER · RAY FLOWER

Daisy

Red Clover Flower

Dandelion Flower

Red Clover

Dandelion

SOME FAMILIES OF FLOWERING PLANTS

After flowering plants first appeared some 130 million years ago, they rapidly "took the earth." Now there are more kinds of flowering plants than of all other plants put together. There are perhaps as many as 200,000 species. They belong in several hundred plant families. In some families there are hundreds of species; in others there are only a few.

Scientists study chiefly the flowers of a flowering plant to find out to what other flowering plants it is closely related. Without a study of their flowers it is hard to see why, for example, the wild rose and the apple belong in the same family or why the onion and the Easter lily are cousins. This chart names some of the many families of flowering plants and shows a few of the plants that belong in those families.

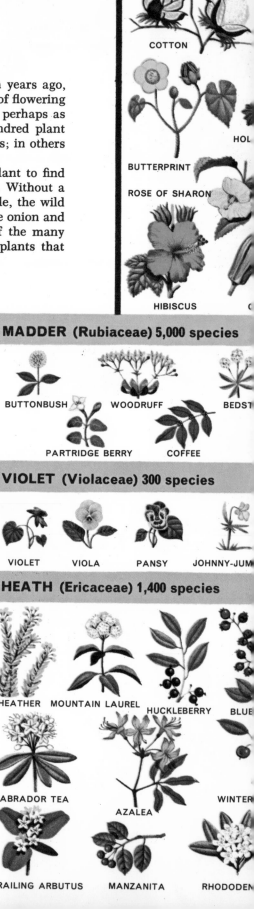

MALLOW (Malvac 1,000 species

COTTON

HOL

BUTTERPRINT

ROSE OF SHARON

HIBISCUS

PALM (Palmaceae) 1,200-1,500 species

PALMETTO

COCONUT PALM

DATE PALM

ROYAL PALM

MADDER (Rubiaceae) 5,000 species

BUTTONBUSH   WOODRUFF   BEDST

PARTRIDGE BERRY   COFFEE

VIOLET (Violaceae) 300 species

VIOLET   VIOLA   PANSY   JOHNNY-JUM

HEATH (Ericaceae) 1,400 species

HEATHER   MOUNTAIN LAUREL   HUCKLEBERRY   BLUE

LABRADOR TEA

AZALEA   WINTER

TRAILING ARBUTUS   MANZANITA   RHODODEN

SE (Rosaceae) 2,500 species

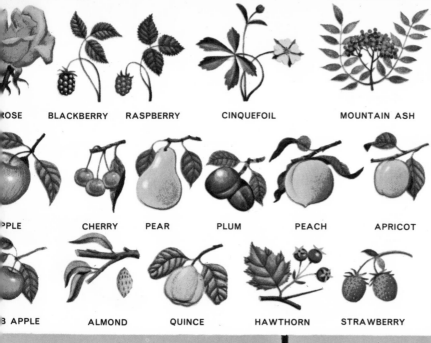

ROSE BLACKBERRY RASPBERRY CINQUEFOIL MOUNTAIN ASH

PPLE CHERRY PEAR PLUM PEACH APRICOT

B APPLE ALMOND QUINCE HAWTHORN STRAWBERRY

MORNING-GLORY (Convolvulaceae) 1,000 species

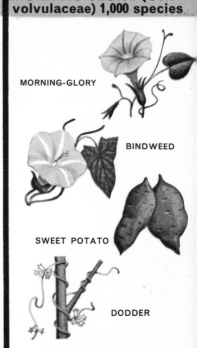

MORNING-GLORY

BINDWEED

SWEET POTATO

DODDER

JE (Rutaceae) 900 species

MQUAT LEMON LIME

PEFRUIT TANGERINE ORANGE WAFER ASH

A (Theaceae) More than 200 species

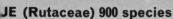

TEA FRANKLINIA TREE CAMELLIA

ASS (Poaceae) 7,000 species

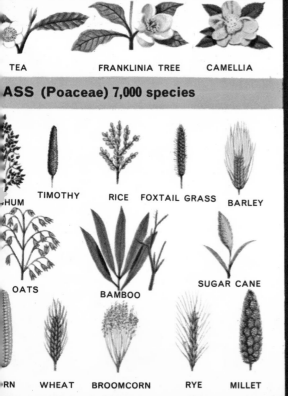

HUM TIMOTHY RICE FOXTAIL GRASS BARLEY

OATS BAMBOO SUGAR CANE

RN WHEAT BROOMCORN RYE MILLET

PEA (Leguminosae) 12,000 species

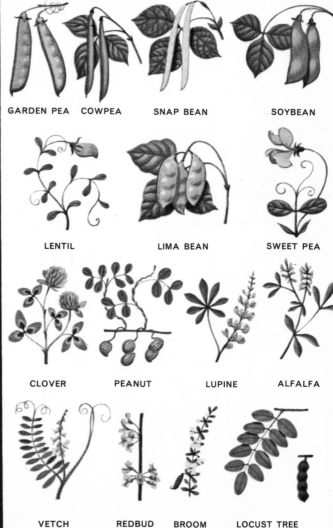

GARDEN PEA COWPEA SNAP BEAN SOYBEAN

LENTIL LIMA BEAN SWEET PEA

CLOVER PEANUT LUPINE ALFALFA

VETCH REDBUD BROOM LOCUST TREE

NIGHTSHADE (Solanaceae) 1,700 species

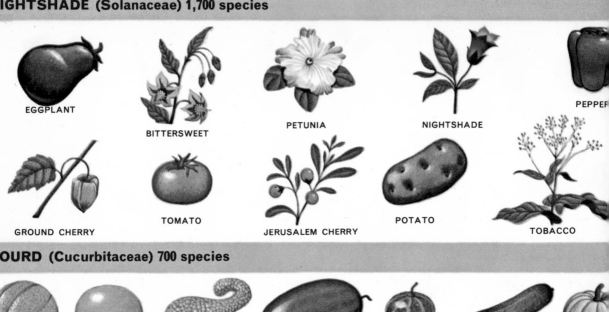

EGGPLANT

BITTERSWEET

PETUNIA

NIGHTSHADE

PEPPER

GROUND CHERRY

TOMATO

JERUSALEM CHERRY

POTATO

TOBACCO

GOURD (Cucurbitaceae) 700 species

CANTALOUPE   HONEYDEW MELON   SQUASH   WATERMELON   GOURD   CUCUMBER   PUMPK

OLIVE (Oleaceae) 500 species

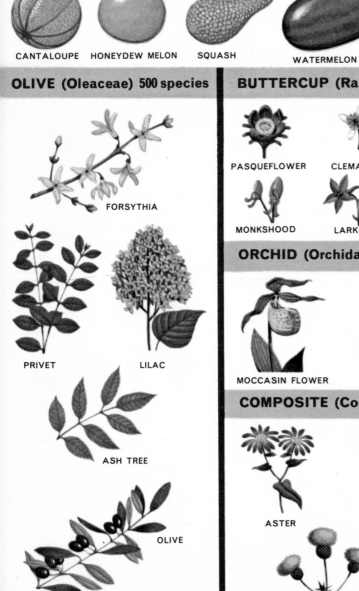

FORSYTHIA

PRIVET

LILAC

ASH TREE

OLIVE

page 90

BUTTERCUP (Ranunculaceae) 1,200 species

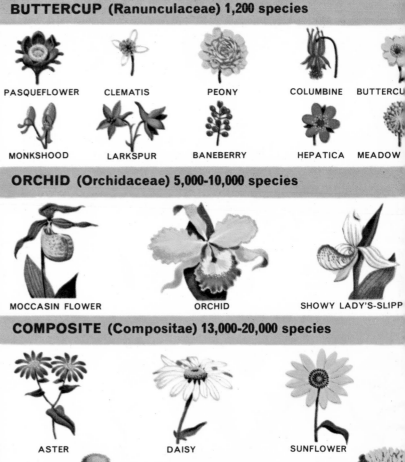

PASQUEFLOWER   CLEMATIS   PEONY   COLUMBINE   BUTTERCU

MONKSHOOD   LARKSPUR   BANEBERRY   HEPATICA   MEADOW

ORCHID (Orchidaceae) 5,000-10,000 species

MOCCASIN FLOWER   ORCHID   SHOWY LADY'S-SLIPP

COMPOSITE (Compositae) 13,000-20,000 species

ASTER   DAISY   SUNFLOWER

CANADA THISTLE   LETTUCE   MARIGOLD

STARD (Cruciferae) 2,000 species

CABBAGE   BRUSSELS SPROUTS   RADISH   TURNIP   STOCK   WATERCRESS

KOHLRABI

MUSTARD   RAPE   SWEET ALYSSUM   KALE   HORSERADISH   PEPPERGRASS

RSLEY (Umbelliferae) 2,500 species

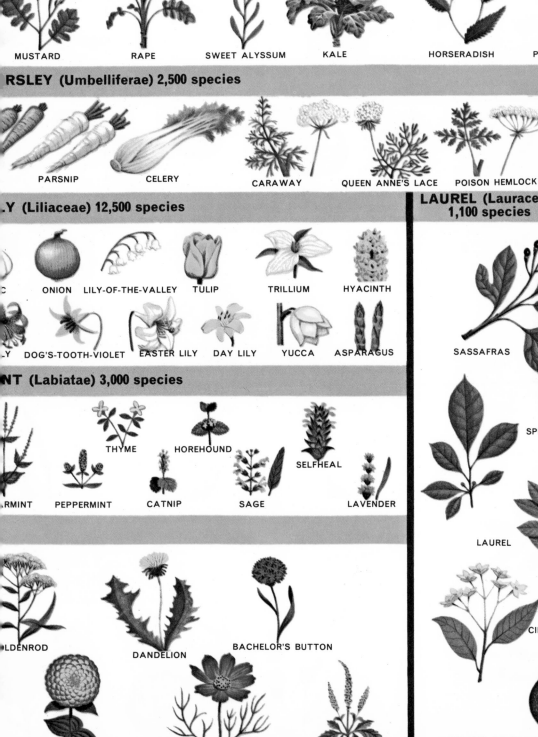

PARSNIP   CELERY   CARAWAY   QUEEN ANNE'S LACE   POISON HEMLOCK   PARSLEY

LY (Liliaceae) 12,500 species

ONION LILY-OF-THE-VALLEY TULIP   TRILLIUM   HYACINTH

LY DOG'S-TOOTH-VIOLET EASTER LILY DAY LILY YUCCA ASPARAGUS

NT (Labiatae) 3,000 species

THYME   HOREHOUND

SELFHEAL

RMINT PEPPERMINT CATNIP   SAGE   LAVENDER

LDENROD   DANDELION   BACHELOR'S BUTTON

ZINNIA   COSMOS   RAGWEED

LAUREL (Lauraceae) 1,100 species

SASSAFRAS

SPICEBUSH

LAUREL

CINNAMON TREE

AVOCADO, OR ALLIGATOR PEAR

STATE FLOWERS
OF THE UNITED STATES

1 ALABAMA—Camellia

2 ALASKA—Forget-me-not

3 ARIZONA—Saguaro

4 ARKANSAS—Apple blossom

5 CALIFORNIA—Golden poppy

6 COLORADO—Columbine

7 CONNECTICUT—Mountain laurel

8 DELAWARE—Peach blossom

9 FLORIDA—Orange blossom

10 GEORGIA—Cherokee rose

11 HAWAII—Hibiscus

12 IDAHO—Syringa (Mock orange)

13 ILLINOIS—Violet

14 INDIANA—Peony

15 IOWA—Wild rose

16 KANSAS—Sunflower

17 KENTUCKY—Goldenrod

18 LOUISIANA—Magnolia

19 MAINE—White pine cone and tassel

20 MARYLAND—Black-eyed Susan

21 MASSACHUSETTS—Trailing arbutus
(Mayflower)

22 MICHIGAN—Apple blossom

23 MINNESOTA—Lady's-slipper

24 MISSISSIPPI—Magnolia

25 MISSOURI—Hawthorn

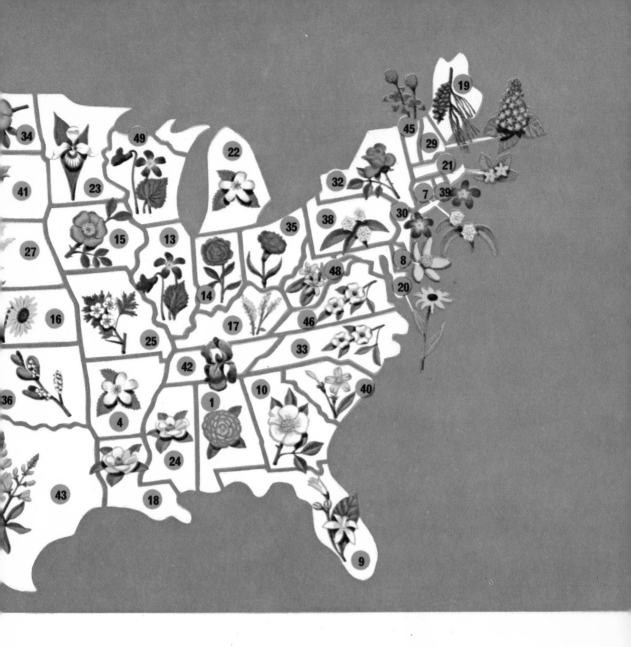

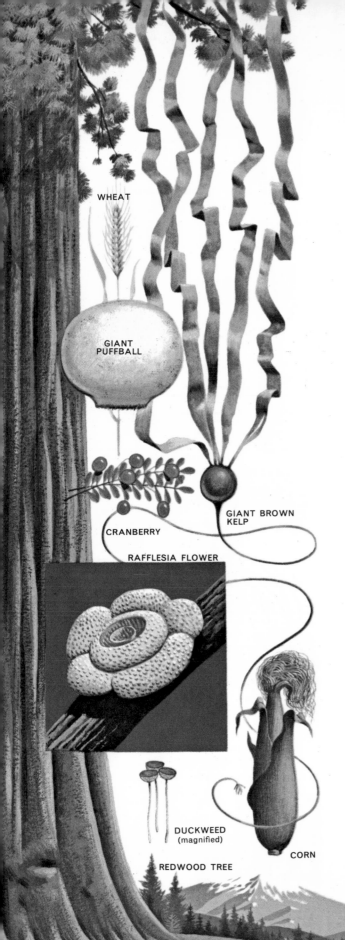

WHEAT

GIANT
PUFFBALL

CRANBERRY

GIANT BROWN
KELP

RAFFLESIA FLOWER

DUCKWEED
(magnified)

CORN

REDWOOD TREE

SOME PLANT FIGURES

Many redwood trees grow to be more than 300 feet tall—taller than a 25-story building. The tallest redwoods are the world's tallest trees. The record height is 364 feet.

A giant brown kelp, a kind of seaweed, may grow to be longer than the tallest of the redwood trees is tall.

Eucalyptus trees are close runners-up of the redwoods. The tallest measured stretches upward 326 feet.

A banyan tree may have as many as a thousand trunks. One banyan tree in India is so big that 7,000 people can stand under it at the same time.

Giant sequoias, or big trees, are so big that the trunk of a single tree could be cut up into enough lumber to build a whole village. Some big trees are thought to be about 4,000 years old. They are among the oldest, if not the very oldest, of all living things.

There are from 800 to 1,000 strands of silk on an ear of corn.

Cranberry plants produce from 4 to 20 million blossoms per acre.

The smallest duckweeds are so tiny that it takes 25 of them to make a row an inch long. Yet these little plants bloom. So far as anyone knows, they are the smallest of all the many thousands of flowering plants.

One of the rafflesias, plants that grow on tropical islands in the Pacific, has flowers that may be more than a yard across. They are not beautiful, and they have a bad odor.

A giant puffball may have trillions of spores inside. If each spore lived and grew into a giant puffball which produced trillions of spores that grew into puffballs, the puffballs in this second generation would take up several hundred times as much space as the earth takes up.

The macrozamia tree of Australia may live to be hundreds or even thousands of years old. After one of these trees is cut down, it may not be completely dead for several years.

A single plant of winter rye grass may have 2 million feet of roots and 6,000 miles of root hairs.

It takes a ton of water to grow the plants that produce a pound of wheat.

PLANT ODDITIES

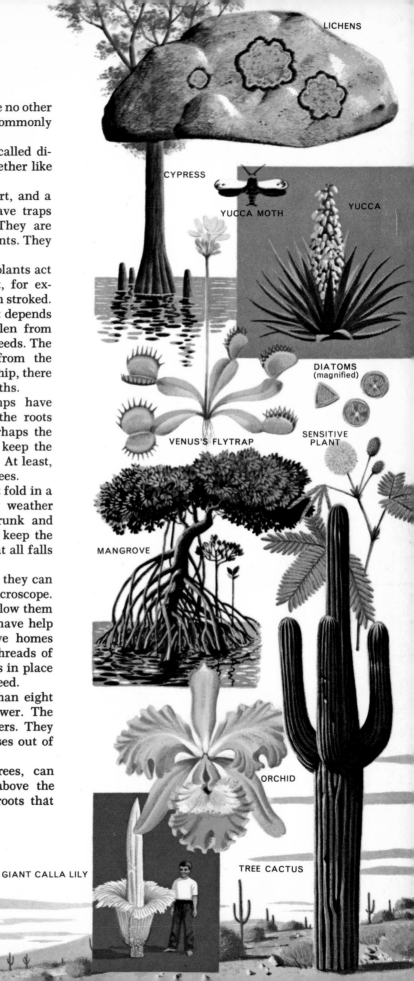

Lichens can grow on bare rocks where no other plants can get a foothold. They are commonly called plant pioneers.

The tiny one-celled green plants called diatoms have glassy shells that fit together like the halves of a pillbox.

Venus's flytrap, sundew, butterwort, and a number of other kinds of plants have traps which are used to catch insects. They are called carnivorous (meat-eating) plants. They use the insects as food.

No plants have nerves. But some plants act as if they had. The sensitive plant, for example, folds up its leaves tightly when stroked.

The yucca of our southwest desert depends on the yucca moth to carry its pollen from flower to flower and thus help form seeds. The yucca-moth caterpillars get food from the yucca. If it were not for this partnership, there would soon be no yucca plants or moths.

Cypress trees growing in swamps have strange knees that grow up from the roots above the surface of the water. Perhaps the knees take in air for the roots and keep the trees from drowning; no one is sure. At least, upland cypress trees do not have knees.

A tree cactus has fluted stems that fold in a little like an accordion during dry weather and swell out after a rain. The trunk and branches can hold enough water to keep the tree alive for a year even if no rain at all falls in the region.

Most orchid seeds are so tiny that they can be seen separately only with a microscope. They are so light that the wind can blow them about like dust. Orchid seeds must have help in starting to grow. In their native homes this help is given by the colorless threads of a fungus. The threads hold the seeds in place and help them get the water they need.

A giant calla lily may be more than eight feet tall. But it is not a single flower. The sheath hides hundreds of tiny flowers. They are on the base of the shaft that rises out of the protecting sheath.

Mangrove trees, unlike most trees, can stand salt water. They are held above the water of coastal swamps by prop roots that look a little like stilts.

LICHENS

CYPRESS

YUCCA MOTH

YUCCA

DIATOMS (magnified)

VENUS'S FLYTRAP

SENSITIVE PLANT

MANGROVE

ORCHID

GIANT CALLA LILY

TREE CACTUS

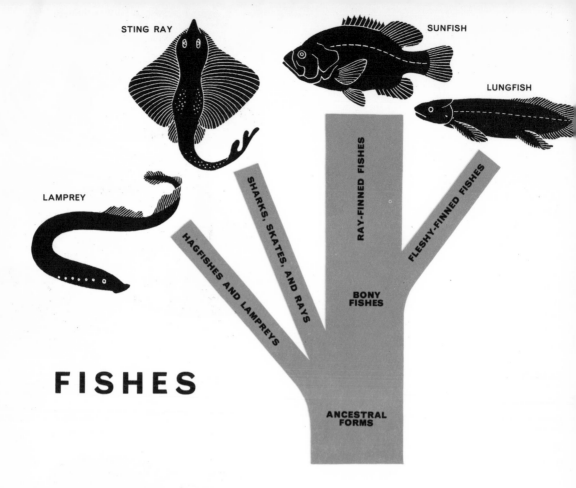

STING RAY

SUNFISH

LUNGFISH

LAMPREY

HAGFISHES AND LAMPREYS

SHARKS, SKATES, AND RAYS

RAY-FINNED FISHES

FLESHY-FINNED FISHES

BONY FISHES

FISHES

ANCESTRAL FORMS

FISH FACTS

Fishes are vertebrates, but some have skeletons of cartilage rather than of bone.

Fishes are cold-blooded.

All fishes have gills; lungfishes have lungs in addition to gills.

All true fishes have fins. Many have two pairs which correspond to our arms and legs.

Most fishes are covered with scales when they are adults.

Rings in the scales of a fish tell the fish's age just as rings in the wood of a tree trunk tell the age of the tree.

Fishes swim chiefly by moving their tails and tail fins from side to side. Their other fins help in steering and balancing.

Many fishes have a swim bladder filled with air. Changing the amount of air in its swim bladder helps a fish go up or down in the water.

A fish's heart has only two chambers.

Most fishes hatch from eggs, but some are live-bearing.

All fishes live in water; some live in salt water, some live in fresh water, and some spend part of their lives in fresh water and part in salt water.

Although all fishes are water animals, some, especially the lungfishes, have ways of surviving when the streams and ponds in which they live dry up.

Fishes have no external ears. Their internal ears are deep within their brain cases.

Some ray-finned fishes are called spiny-rayed fishes because of sharp spines in some of their fins. The perch is a typical spiny-rayed fish.

Fishes cannot close their eyes; they have no eyelids.

With the sense organs along its lateral line, a fish can sense movement and changes in pressure in the water surrounding it.

Many fishes make noises—drones, croaks, grunts, cackles, squawks, purrs, etc. Fish noises can be picked up with a hydrophone.

Some fishes live in very cold water. Scientists have blasted holes in antarctic ice to collect fishes from the water under the ice.

The food of most fishes can be traced back to diatoms, microscopic green plants.

The first fishes appeared on the earth long before any other animals with backbones.

Many of the fishes of past ages had armor.

FISH FIGURES

Fishes form the largest group of backboned animals. There are at least 20,000 species.

The ling, or mud hake, is a relative of the common cod. This fish is famous for the number of eggs it lays—about 28 million at a time. But fewer than one in a million hatch and live to grow up.

A kind of goby found in the Philippines is one of the smallest, if not the very smallest, fish in the world. It is less than half an inch long when full grown.

The whale shark is the largest of all fishes. A whale shark may be 45 feet long and weigh 50 tons. Some sharks are man-eaters, but the whale shark is harmless. It eats very small animals which it strains from the sea water it swims in.

The most common fish in the sea is one which a great many people have never seen or even heard of. It is a deep-water fish called the bristlemouth.

Less than 1⁄50 of all the kinds of fishes known in the world are now being used as food, for their oil, or as fertilizer.

In the United States the total annual fish "harvest" amounts to about five billion pounds.

The total annual catch of fish in the whole world is about 30 million tons. More than 95 per cent of this catch is made in the waters of the northern hemisphere.

Herring, like many other fishes, swim in schools, or shoals. One shoal of herring is likely to have from half a billion to three billion herring in it. About ten billion are caught

GOBY

WHALE SHARK

every year. The herring is considered the world's most important food fish.

The fish who live half a mile down in the ocean stand a pressure of more than 1,000 pounds on every square inch of their bodies.

A species of fish can hold its own if only two of the offspring of every female fish survive.

Some fishes make journeys of thousands of miles. The eel is one of them.

Some fishes are very fast swimmers. The blue marlin can swim 50 miles an hour—faster than a horse can run. There are fishes even faster—for example, the swordfish and the sailfish.

There have been fishes on the earth for at least 400 million years.

PARTS OF A SPINY-RAYED FISH

Operculum or Gill Cover
Lateral Line
Spiny Dorsal Fin
Soft Dorsal Fin
Nostrils
Pectoral Fin
Ventral Fins
Scales
Anal Fin
Caudal or Tail Fin

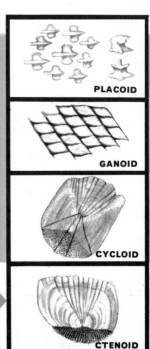

PLACOID

GANOID

CYCLOID

CTENOID

TYPES OF FISH SCALES

SEA HORSE

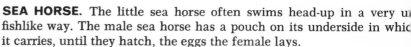

SOME
"QUEER FISH"

FLYING FISH

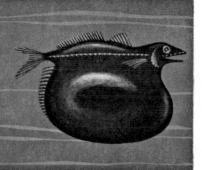

ARCHER FISH

BLACK SWALLOWER

CLIMBING PERCH

SEA HORSE. The little sea horse often swims head-up in a very u[n]fishlike way. The male sea horse has a pouch on its underside in whic[h] it carries, until they hatch, the eggs the female lays.

ARCHER FISH. The little archer fish of Asia gets its name from th[e] strange way in which it catches its food. It "shoots" the insects it eat[s]. Its arrow is a stream of water which it shoots out of its mouth.

BLACK SWALLOWER. The black swallower is a tiny deep-sea fish. Th[is] fish eats other fish, and it often swallows a fish much bigger than itsel[f]. Both its mouth and its stomach can stretch enormously.

CLIMBING PERCH. A climbing perch is not as "lost" out of water as [a] fish is supposed to be. This little fish of Asia has a way of holding wat[er] around its gills so that it can stay out of water for some time.

SWORDFISH. A full-grown swordfish may weigh half a ton and be 1[5] feet long. The sword which gives this fish its name may be more than [a] yard long and strong enough to pierce a small boat.

SAILFISH. The sailfish has a sword, but this fish is much smaller tha[n] a swordfish. Not many sailfishes weigh more than 100 pounds. The sai[l]fish is one of the fastest fishes, and one of the most beautiful.

OCEAN SUNFISH. The ocean sunfish is often called the headfish, f[or] it is almost all head. A full-grown headfish may weigh more than 60[0] pounds. As one would guess from its shape, the ocean sunfish is not at a[ll] a fast swimmer.

ELECTRIC EEL. Several fishes can give electric shocks to any enem[y] attacking them. The fish that gives the most powerful shocks to its e[n]emies is the electric eel of South America. Its shock can stun a horse.

GAFFTOPSAIL CATFISH. This catfish has a strange way of guardin[g] its eggs. After the eggs are laid, the male fish gathers them up in h[is] mouth. He carries them there until they hatch. For weeks he cannot ea[t].

ANGLER. The anglers get their name from the "fishing rods" they car[ry] around on their heads. The angler pictured lives in the deep sea. Th[e] "bait" on its fishing rod is luminous.

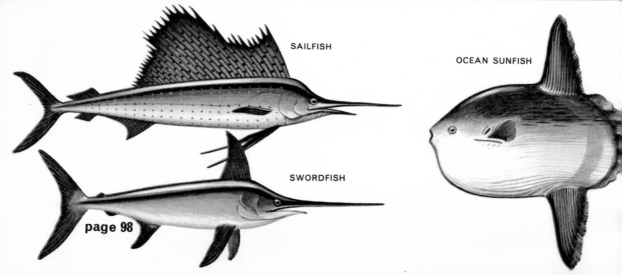

SAILFISH

OCEAN SUNFISH

SWORDFISH

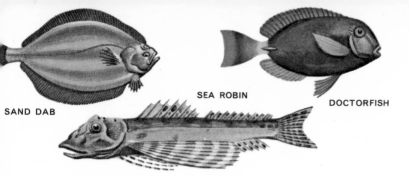

SAND DAB

SEA ROBIN

DOCTORFISH

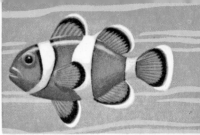

CLOWN FISH

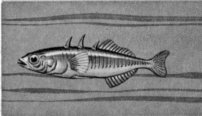

STICKLEBACK

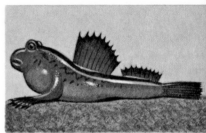

MUDSKIPPER

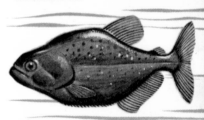

PIRANHA

FOUR-EYES

FLYING FISH. The flying fish cannot really fly. By moving its tail rapidly it sends itself swiftly along the surface of the water. Its two big fins then act as wings to help it glide upward and perhaps escape an enemy.

SAND DAB. The sand dab is a flatfish. All the flatfishes swim about and lie on the ocean floor on their sides. Both their eyes are on the side that is uppermost. The sand dab is so thin that light can shine through it.

SEA ROBIN. The sea robin is sometimes called the "walking fish." Its "legs," which are a part of its pectoral fins, serve as feelers for finding food on the sea bottom. It finds worms and shellfish there.

DOCTORFISH. The doctorfish, or common surgeon, gets its name from two spines that are as sharp as a doctor's lancet. These two spines are on the fish's sides just in front of its tail.

CLOWN FISH. The clown fish has formed a partnership with certain kinds of sea anemones. The sea anemones, with their stinging cells, protect the fish from its enemies. In exchange for this protection the clown fish brings food to the anemones.

STICKLEBACK. Most fishes that lay eggs lay their eggs and then leave them. But some fishes build nests for their eggs and guard the nests. The small stickleback is one of the nest-building fishes.

MUDSKIPPER. This little fish, which lives along the shores of West Africa, spends much time perching on rocks or tree roots at the edge of the water. It can walk, run, and even jump with its fins and tail.

PIRANHA. This fish of the Amazon River has teeth that can make nicks in steel. It has the reputation of being one of the fiercest of all fishes. Another name for the piranha is "tiger fish."

FOUR-EYES. The four-eyes gets its name from the fact that each of its eyes is divided into two parts. As the fish swims along the surface, the upper parts of its eyes see above the surface, the lower parts below it.

PORCUPINE FISH. The spines of a porcupine fish serve to protect it from its enemies. A porcupine fish, moreover, can puff itself up so that it is too big for some of its enemies to swallow.

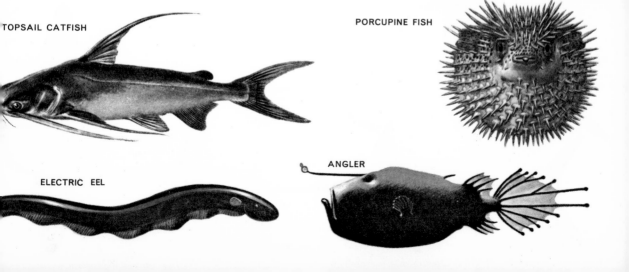

TOPSAIL CATFISH

PORCUPINE FISH

ELECTRIC EEL

ANGLER

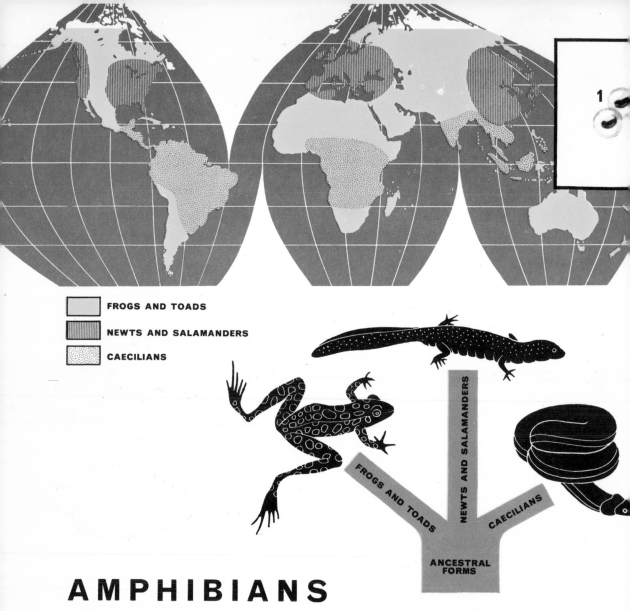

FROGS AND TOADS

NEWTS AND SALAMANDERS

CAECILIANS

NEWTS AND SALAMANDERS

FROGS AND TOADS

CAECILIANS

ANCESTRAL FORMS

AMPHIBIANS

Amphibians are vertebrates; they all have backbones.

Amphibians have no scales, fur, or feathers; their skins are bare.

Like all animals except birds and mammals, amphibians are cold-blooded. Those that live in regions with cold winters hibernate.

"Amphibian" means "living in two places." As a rule amphibians live in water and breathe with gills when young. When grown most of them live on land and breathe with lungs or through their skin. Some, like the mud puppy, never grow up to be air-breathing animals.

There are about 2,000 species of amphibians. Of these about 60 are caecilians, about 200 are newts or salamanders, and the rest are toads or frogs.

Newts and salamanders have both legs and tails when grown. Toads and frogs have legs

but, as a rule, no tails. Caecilians have no legs and only very short tails.

There are no amphibians, young or old, in the sea.

Almost all amphibians hatch from eggs; only one kind is known to be born.

Many amphibians change greatly in appearance as they grow up. Young toads and frogs are called tadpoles. Young amphibians of other kinds are usually called larvas.

Amphibians must have moist surroundings. There is no truth in the old belief that a salamander could live even in a blazing fire.

The largest amphibian is the two-foot-long giant salamander of Japan.

The smallest amphibians are the tree toads.

The earliest four-legged animals were amphibians. Amphibians were the first animals to have voices.

Life History of a Typical Amphibian

THE FISH THAT WALKED

The amphibians are descendants of the fishes. The first amphibian is often spoken of as "the fish that walked." Scientists believe that the move from water to land came about in some such way as this: Long dry periods made life difficult for the fish in ponds and streams and shallow seas. The water became foul, and it was hard for the fish to get enough oxygen. The simple lungs which some fishes of the time had were a big help. To escape from the foul water for a little while, the fishes with lungs would flop up on land and breathe with their lungs. Of course, their fins were not good for land travel. But generation by generation their fins grew stouter until finally they were stubby legs. At the same time their lungs grew better. The creatures lost many of their fish characteristics and were air-breathing animals that could live a large part of their lives on land; they were amphibians.

THE PUZZLING AXOLOTL

"Axolotl" is an Aztec word meaning "servant of water." The name was given long ago to a salamander found in mountain lakes of Mexico and western United States. As the people who gave it a name knew it, this salamander, like the mud puppy, never grew up. Even though it produced young, it kept its larval shape and its gills and continued to live in water. Now scientists have found that the axolotl is merely the larval form of the tiger salamander. In the eastern part of the United States this salamander follows the usual salamander pattern of spending its early life in water and its later life as an air-breathing animal on land. Scientists have found that occasionally a western axolotl will follow this pattern. Why the life-histories as a rule differ in the different regions is puzzling.

A GIANT AMPHIBIAN OF LONG AGO

Millions of years ago there were amphibians much larger than any amphibians of today. One of these big amphibians was *Eryops*. *Eryops* was over 8 feet long and had a head 18 inches across. Its mouth was enormous. Scientists believe from the fossils of this ancient amphibian that *Eryops*, like many of its relatives, had three eyes—two in the usual place and one in the top of its head.

The legs of *Eryops* were very short; they did not hold the creature far above the ground. Probably it spent most of its time sunning itself near the edge of a swamp or pond and waiting for a fish to be washed up on shore or for a smaller amphibian or a reptile to come close enough to be caught. Probably *Eryops* ate some insects, too; there were many big insects in its time.

ERYOPS

REPTILES OF TODAY

There are at least five thousand kinds of reptiles living now.

Reptiles are vertebrates; they have backbones. Like fishes, amphibians, and all invertebrates, they are cold blooded.

Reptiles breathe with lungs all their lives. They do not at any time breathe with gills. Every cold-blooded animal that has a backbone but never has gills is a reptile.

The word "reptile" means "crawling animal." But not all reptiles crawl, and not all animals that crawl are reptiles.

Different groups of reptiles differ greatly in appearance. Turtles have legs and shells; alligators and crocodiles have legs but no shells; snakes have no legs and no shells. Most lizards have legs, but a few do not. None of them have shells.

The tuatara looks much like a lizard, but it differs from the lizards enough to make scientists put it in an order all by itself. The tuatara has the longest history of any reptile of today. It has been on the earth almost unchanged for more than 200 million years. Now it is found only on islands near New Zealand. It grows to be about two feet long.

The alligators and crocodiles are on the average bigger than the turtles, lizards, or snakes.

Reptiles, with very few exceptions, are covered with scales. Contrary to the belief of most people, they are not slimy.

By far the greatest number of reptiles are land animals; even those that live in water come on land to lay their eggs.

Most reptiles lay eggs, but some snakes carry their eggs inside their bodies until the young snakes develop. The little snakes are then born.

Reptiles are far more common in warm regions than in those with cold winters. The snakes and lizards found in regions of cold winters must hibernate.

All alligators, crocodiles, and snakes are meat eaters. The tuatara is a meat eater, too; it eats chiefly insects. Most lizards are meat eaters, but some are vegetarians. Turtles eat both plant and animal food.

Snakes have no eyelids. They have forked tongues; so do some lizards.

Turtles have no teeth.

Today reptiles rank in importance to us far below the fishes, birds, and mammals.

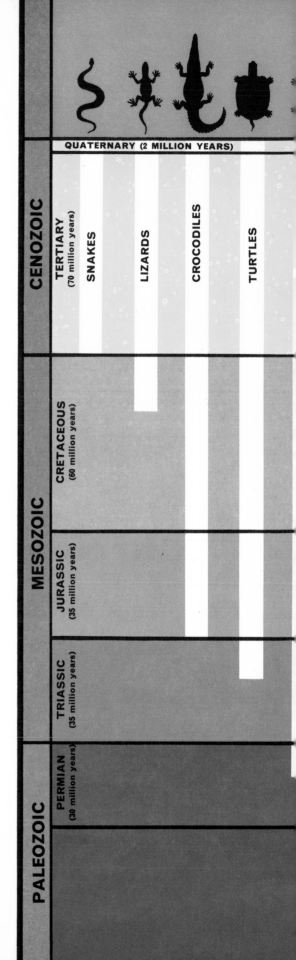

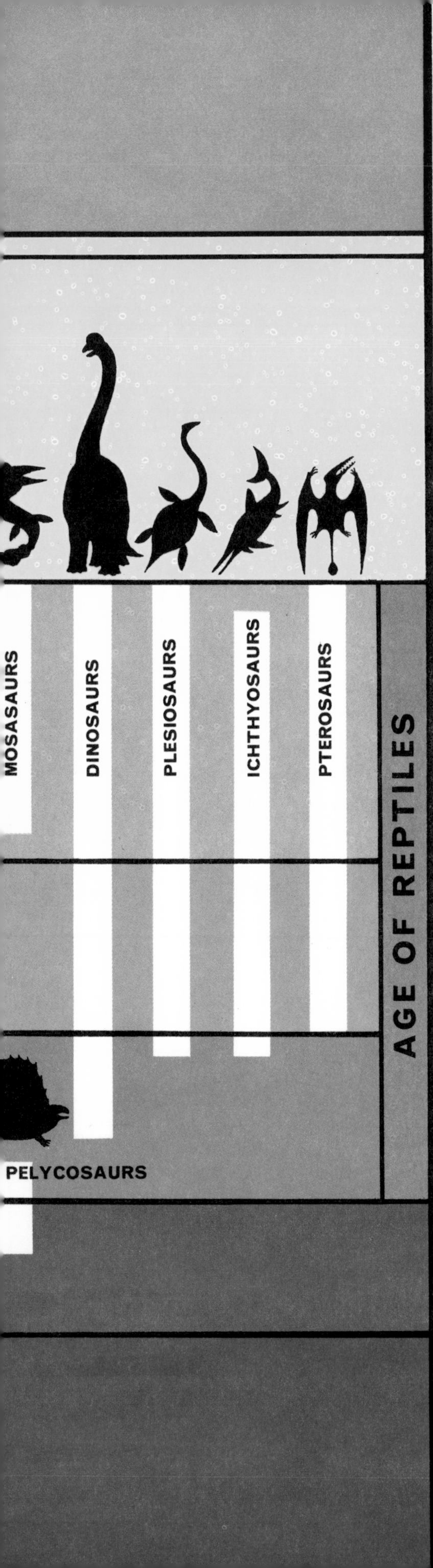

MOSASAURS

DINOSAURS

PLESIOSAURS

ICHTHYOSAURS

PTEROSAURS

AGE OF REPTILES

PELYCOSAURS

REPTILES OF LONG AGO

For many millions of years reptiles were the earth's leading animals. The time is called the Age of Reptiles. Several groups of reptiles that were very common then are wholly extinct.

Among the early reptiles were the *pelycosaurs*. Some of them had great "sails" growing upward from their backs. In spite of their sails, these reptiles lived on land.

The *plesiosaurs* were reptiles of the sea. A plesiosaur had a broad, rather flat body somewhat like a turtle's. But as a rule it had an extremely long unturtlelike neck and a small head. Its legs were paddles. The largest of these marine reptiles were 50 feet long, but most of them were not more than half that length. They were not fast swimmers, but, with their long, sharp teeth, they were good hunters. The plesiosaurs did not become extinct until near the close of the Age of Reptiles some 70 million years ago.

The name *ichthyosaur* means "fish reptile." As the picture shows, the name fits well. The ichthyosaurs were far bigger than most fishes of today. Some were 25 feet long or even longer. They were rapid swimmers and could leap high into the air. Even though these fish reptiles seem to have been well fitted for living in the sea, all of them disappeared before the end of the Age of Reptiles.

The *mosasaurs* were ancient marine lizards. Fossils of them have been found in many different parts of the world. The biggest mosasaurs were from 30 to 40 feet long. They were perhaps the fiercest of the reptiles that lived in the sea. These marine lizards were common late in the Age of Reptiles.

During the Age of Reptiles there were reptiles in the air as well as on land and in the water. The flying reptiles—the *pterosaurs* (winged reptiles), or *pterodactyls* (wingfingers)—had big wings. *Pteranodon*, the last of the pterosaurs, had a wingspread of nearly 30 feet! Birds descended from the reptiles but not from the flying reptiles. The pterosaurs left no descendants to live on after the Age of Reptiles.

By far the best known of the reptiles that ruled the earth during the Age of Reptiles were the *dinosaurs*. The biggest dinosaurs were the largest animals that ever walked on land. The disappearance of the dinosaurs marked the end of the Age of Reptiles.

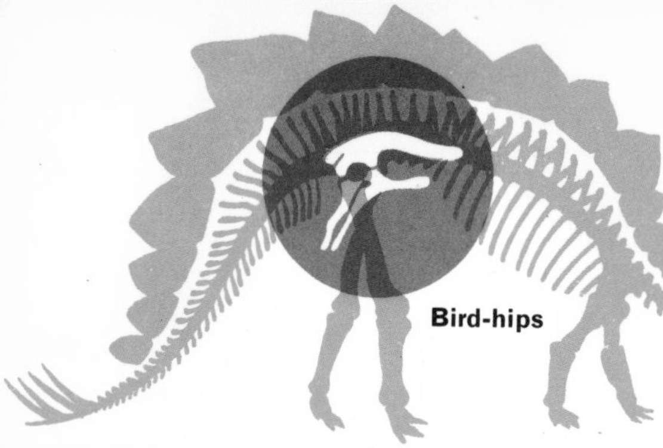

Bird-hips

DINOSAUR

Dinosaurs are divided
two orders—the **Sauris**
or "reptile-hips" and
Ornithischia or "bird-h

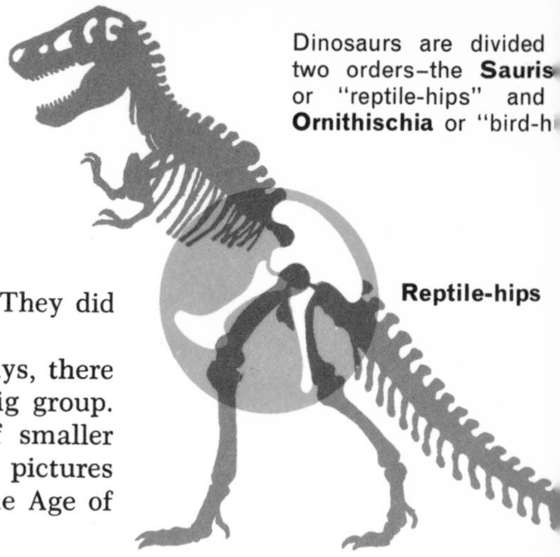

Reptile-hips

There were at least five thousand kinds of dinosaurs. They did not, however, all live at the same time.

Although the dinosaurs were all alike in certain ways, there were many differences among the members of this big group. Scientists have divided the group into a number of smaller groups. The chart below shows the main groups and pictures one dinosaur in each group. It shows, too, when in the Age of Reptiles each group flourished.

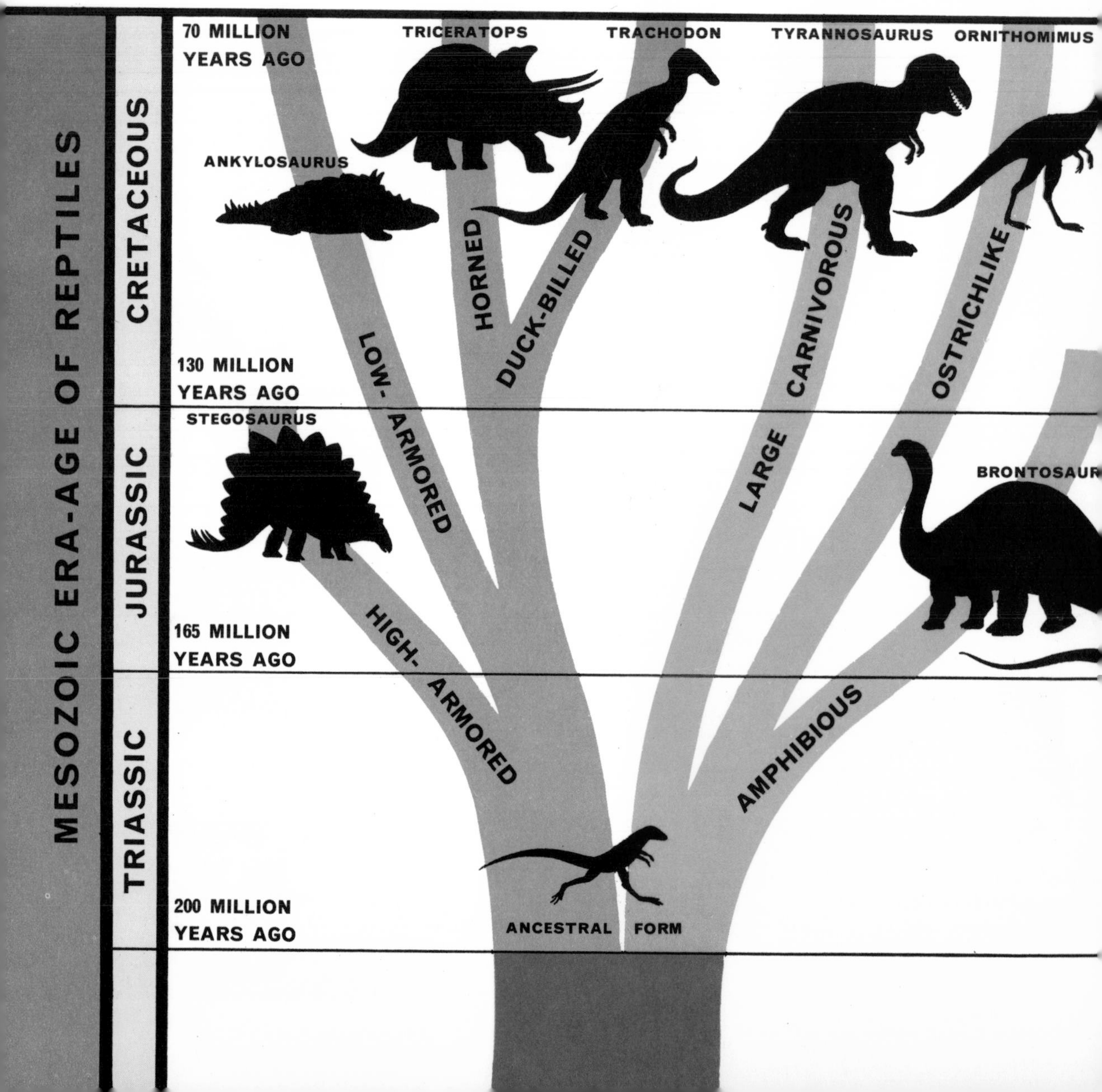

MESOZOIC ERA-AGE OF REPTILES

CRETACEOUS

70 MILLION YEARS AGO

TRICERATOPS TRACHODON TYRANNOSAURUS ORNITHOMIMUS

ANKYLOSAURUS

HORNED DUCK-BILLED LARGE CARNIVOROUS OSTRICHLIKE

LOW-ARMORED

130 MILLION YEARS AGO

JURASSIC

STEGOSAURUS

BRONTOSAUR

HIGH-ARMORED

165 MILLION YEARS AGO

TRIASSIC

AMPHIBIOUS

ANCESTRAL FORM

200 MILLION YEARS AGO

The earliest dinosaurs walked on two legs. The fossil footprints of these dinosaurs were first thought to be the footprints of great birds. Some dinosaurs ate plants. Others ate meat.

The largest dinosaurs were far larger than any land animals of today. They were not, however, nearly as big as whales. Although some dinosaurs were gigantic, there were small dinosaurs, too. Some were no bigger than chickens. Some dinosaurs were very clumsy and slow-moving; others were quick and agile.

No dinosaur had much room in its head for brains. In its 35-ton body, *Brontosaurus*, the thunder lizard, had a brain weighing about a pound.

Some dinosaurs had very thick skulls, so thick that these dinosaurs deserve to be called "boneheads."

The amphibious dinosaurs got this name because they are supposed to have spent much of their time in swamps and lagoons where the water helped them support their great weight. The largest of the dinosaurs belonged in this group.

Brachiosaurus is supposed to have been the largest of all dinosaurs. A full-grown *Brachiosaurus* weighed as much as six or seven hundred people. Dinosaurs of this kind were about 80 feet long. Eight of them marching nose to tip of tail would have made a procession as long as a city block.

Diplodocus, although not so heavy as *Brontosaurus* and *Brachiosaurus*, was longer. It grew to be nearly 90 feet long. This dinosaur, and many others, had a kind of "second brain," a great swelling of the spinal cord at the base of the tail. This "second brain" controlled the movements of the animal's tail and legs. Such an arrangement was very fortunate for an animal as long as *Diplodocus*. Suppose a meat eater had caught *Diplodocus* by the end of the tail. If a nerve message had had to go all the way to the true brain of *Diplodocus* and a message to move had had to come back, it would have taken many seconds—long enough for *Diplodocus* to be badly hurt.

Stegosaurus, a plant eater, was protected somewhat from the meat eaters of its time by the double row of plates down its back. But the plates were not a complete protection, for fossil bones of *Stegosaurus* have been found bearing toothmarks of a meat-eating dinosaur.

Some horned dinosaurs had more elaborate frills of bone protecting their necks than *Triceratops*. Clearly these dinosaurs were most easily attacked from behind.

The low-armored dinosaurs were like armored tanks. Even their legs were protected by bony plates.

Tyrannosaurus was the giant of the meat-eating dinosaurs and was probably the biggest meat-eating land animal of all time. It grew to be from 18 to 20 feet tall. It could open its big mouth a full yard.

Trachodon, a harmless plant eater, was one of the common dinosaurs in the closing stages of the Age of Reptiles.

Some of the duck-billed dinosaurs had great crests on their heads. Perhaps air stored in them made it possible for the dinosaurs to feed under water.

The ostrichlike dinosaurs were about the shape of an ostrich except for their long tails. Of course, they had no feathers. Although birds descended from reptiles, they did not descend from the ostrichlike dinosaurs.

Dinosaurs laid eggs. Fossil eggs of the little horned dinosaur *Protoceratops* have been found.

BRACHIOSAURUS

DIPLODOCUS

STYRACOSAURUS

CORYTHOSAURUS

PROTOCERATOPS

POISONOUS SNAKES

A great many people are afraid of snakes and think that any snake should be killed on sight. Actually most snakes are harmless, and some do a great deal of good by eating such animals as field mice and rats. There are, however, some poisonous snakes, and some are very poisonous indeed. About 10,000 people die each year in India alone from the bites of poisonous snakes, and thousands more die in other tropical regions. Poisonous snakes inject their poison with fangs that are like hypodermic needles.

Deaths from snakebite have been cut down in recent years by the use of antivenins—antitoxins that work against the snake poisons. There are now few deaths from snakebite in the United States, Canada, and European countries.

The only poisonous snakes in the United States are the rattlesnakes, the coral snakes, the water moccasin, and the copperhead. There are many in other lands.

Most of the poisonous snakes of the United States are RATTLESNAKES. There are rattlesnakes of one kind or another in almost every section of the country. The eastern diamondback is the largest rattler and the States' largest poisonous snake. It may be more than eight feet long. Rattlesnakes get their name from the rattles on their tails. A rattlesnake often shakes its rattle when it is about to strike and thus gives a warning.

The COPPERHEAD gets its name from the coppery-brown color of its head. This snake, which is three or four feet long, is found chiefly in the southeastern states, but it may be found in every state east of the Mississippi and in some of the southern states farther west. A copperhead fights very hard if it is trapped.

The WATER MOCCASIN, somewhat longer than the copperhead, is found in the southeastern states. It lives in swampy regions. It belongs, as do also the copperhead and the

WATER MOCCASIN

COMMON CORAL SNAKE

COPPERHEAD

EASTERN DIAMONDBACK

rattlesnakes, to a group of poisonous snakes called pit vipers. They have pits between their eyes and their nostrils which, because they are sensitive to heat, help the snakes tell when they are near a warm-blooded animal. Another name for the water moccasin is "cottonmouth." This name comes from the white lining of the snake's mouth.

The CORAL SNAKES are beautifully colored, but very poisonous. The common coral snake, which is about a yard long, is found in the South. The western coral snake is only about a foot and a half long. The coral snakes do not do as much harm as one would expect, for their fangs are too short to go through heavy cloth or shoe leather.

Of the poisonous snakes of other lands the FER-DE-LANCE is one of the most dangerous. It is another of the pit vipers. This snake is found chiefly in the hot lands of northern South America. It may grow to be eight feet long. The fer-de-lance is a common snake, partly because a mother snake produces so many young—as many as 70 at a time. Within a few minutes from the time they are born the little snakes are able to defend themselves with their poison fangs.

There are a dozen or so kinds of COBRAS. The Indian cobra can be blamed for a great many of the deaths from snakebite in India. The spreading heads of the cobras make them look quite different from most snakes. The Indian cobra, which is about six feet long, is the snake most often used by snake charmers. Kipling's famous story of Rikki-Tikki-Tavi is about an Indian cobra and a mongoose. Some of the cobras found in Africa can actually spit their poison for quite a distance and can blind an approaching enemy. A common way for a person in ancient Egypt to commit suicide was to let an asp—a kind of African cobra—bite him. The king cobra of Siam is the largest of all poisonous snakes; it may be 18 feet long.

The TIGER SNAKE of Australia is a relative of the cobras. A full-grown tiger snake, which is about six feet long, has enough poison in its poison glands to kill 400 people. This snake, like the fer-de-lance, produces a great many young.

The MAMBA of Africa is another relative of the cobras. This snake may be 14 feet long. The natives of Africa are very much afraid of it. When a person comes close, it shows no disposition to run away, and its venom is very deadly.

The GABOON VIPER of Africa belongs to the group of poisonous snakes called the true vipers. It is a huge snake: although it is no longer than the cobras, its body measures six inches across. The poison fangs of this big snake may be an inch and a half long. A famous zoo curator almost lost his life from being bitten by a Gaboon viper. In the regions where it lives, however, this big snake uses its poison almost entirely on animals it needs for food. Few African natives are bitten by it.

The TIC-POLONGA of southeastern Asia is also one of the true vipers. Another name for it is Russell's viper. It is a somewhat smaller snake than the Indian cobra, but is almost as much feared. The tic-polonga would cause far fewer deaths if not so many children went barefoot in the region where it lives.

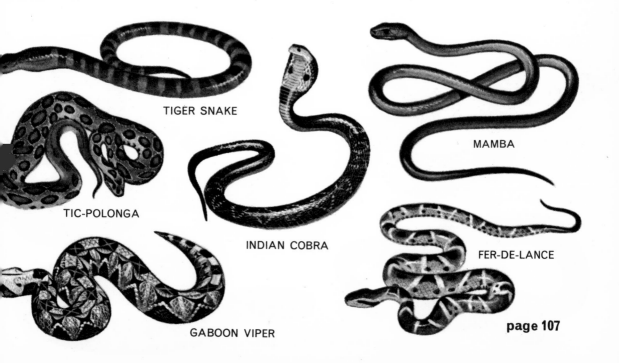

TIGER SNAKE

MAMBA

TIC-POLONGA

INDIAN COBRA

FER-DE-LANCE

GABOON VIPER

BIRDS

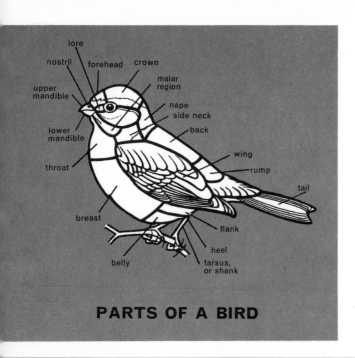

lore
nostril
forehead
crown
malar region
upper mandible
nape
side neck
lower mandible
back
wing
throat
rump
tail
breast
flank
heel
belly
tarsus, or shank

PARTS OF A BIRD

Birds are vertebrates; they all have backbones. Like mammals, they are warm-blooded.

All birds have feathers when grown; and every animal with feathers is a bird.

Birds breathe with lungs all their lives.

All birds have two legs.

All birds have two wings, but in a few species the wings are so reduced in size that they are hidden and useless.

Although as a rule birds can fly, there are a number of species of flightless birds.

All birds come from eggs; there are no live-bearing birds.

Some birds when hatched are covered with down and can run about almost at once; others are naked and very helpless when hatched.

A bird has a heart with four chambers just as a human being has.

No birds of today have teeth.

The normal temperature for a bird may be as high as 112° F.—a temperature that would be a terrifically high fever for a human being.

There are more than 20,000 species of birds. About 1,500 are found in North America.

Birds have been on the earth for at least 150 million years.

THREE FLIGHTLESS GIANTS OF THE PAST

MOA

PHORORHACOS

The tallest moas were about 11 feet tall—taller than any birds of today and any other birds of the past. The "drumstick" of a moa giant was nearly a yard long. The moas lived in New Zealand. They disappeared some four centuries ago.

Phororhacos lived in Patagonia some 20,000,000 years ago. It was as tall as a man and had an enormous head—one as big as the head of a horse. Its beak had a sharp hook good for tearing meat.

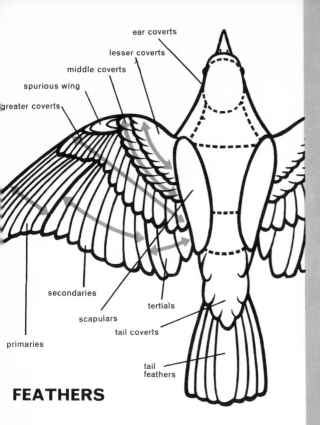

ear coverts

lesser coverts

middle coverts

spurious wing

greater coverts

secondaries

scapulars

tertials

tail coverts

primaries

tail feathers

FEATHERS

AEPYORNIS

Aepyornis lived in Madagascar during the Ice Age. This "elephant bird" was as tall as an ostrich and laid much bigger eggs. They were more than a foot long, the biggest bird eggs anyone knows about.

BIRD ORDERS

 Flightless Birds Cassowaries, Emus, Kiwis, Ostriches, Rheas

 Loons

 Grebes

 Petrels and Albatrosses

 Penguins

 Pelicans and Cormorants

 Herons, Storks, Flamingos, and Bitterns

 Rails, Gallinules, and Cranes

 Gulls, Terns, Sandpipers, Auks, and Plovers

 Ducks, Geese, and Swans

 Grouse, Quail, Pheasants, Turkeys, and Chickens

 Vultures, Hawks, and Eagles

 Owls

 Pigeons and Doves

 Parrots

 Cuckoos and Roadrunners

 Whippoorwills and Nighthawks

 Swifts and Hummingbirds

 Kingfishers and Hornbills

 Woodpeckers and Toucans

 Perching Birds Blackbirds, Cardinals, Chickadees, Crows, Flycatchers, Grosbeaks, Jays, Mockingbirds, Nuthatches, Sparrows, Swallows, Tanagers, Thrushes, Warblers, Wrens

STATE BIRDS
OF THE UNITED STATES

1	ALABAMA - Yellowhammer (Flicker)	**14**	INDIANA - Cardinal
2	ALASKA - Ptarmigan	**15**	IOWA - Goldfinch
3	ARIZONA - Cactus wren	**16**	KANSAS - Western meadowlark
4	ARKANSAS - Mockingbird	**17**	KENTUCKY - Cardinal
5	CALIFORNIA - California quail	**18**	LOUISIANA - Brown pelican
6	COLORADO - Lark bunting	**19**	MAINE - Black-capped chickadee
7	CONNECTICUT - Robin	**20**	MARYLAND - Baltimore oriole
8	DELAWARE - Blue hen chicken	**21**	MASSACHUSETTS - Black-capped chickadee
9	FLORIDA - Mockingbird		
10	GEORGIA - Brown thrasher	**22**	MICHIGAN - Robin
11	HAWAII - Nene (Hawaiian goose)	**23**	MINNESOTA - Loon
12	IDAHO - Mountain bluebird	**24**	MISSISSIPPI - Mockingbird
13	ILLINOIS - Cardinal	**25**	MISSOURI - Eastern bluebird

MAMMALS

Mammals are vertebrates; they all have backbones.

Mammals are warm-blooded.

Mammals feed their young with milk from their own bodies.

Every mammal except a few that have taken to the sea has four limbs.

Mammals, even those which live in water, breathe with lungs all their lives.

There are several thousand species of mammals.

Duckbills and spiny anteaters are hatched from eggs; all other mammals are born.

Mammals are so well known that many people think of them as the only true animals.

Mammals are all large enough to be easily noticeable, and the biggest are the largest animals that have ever lived.

Mammals have hair; some, however, have very little.

Most mammals have two sets of teeth: the "milk" teeth which fall out early in life, and the permanent teeth.

Most mammals have the senses of hearing, touching, tasting, smelling, and seeing well developed.

A mammal's heart has four chambers.

The brains of mammals are well developed.

The first mammals appeared on the earth more than 175 million years ago!

MAMMAL ORDERS

Monotremes
Duckbill, Spiny Anteater

Marsupials
Bandicoots, Kangaroos, Koala, Opossums, Tasmanian Devil, Wombats

Insectivores
Hedgehogs, Moles, Shrews

Carnivores
Bears, Cats, Dogs, Foxes, Hyenas, Lions, Otters, Raccoons, Sea Lions, Seals, Skunks, Tigers, Walruses, Weasels, Wolves

Odd-toed Ungulates
Asses, Horses, Rhinoceroses, Tapirs, Zebras

Even-toed Ungulates
Alpacas, Antelopes, Camels, Cattle, Deer, Giraffes, Goats, Hippopotamuses, Llamas, Pigs, Sheep

Cetaceans
Dolphins, Porpoises, Whales

Elephants

Sea Cows
Dugong, Manatee

Hyraxes

Rodents
Beavers, Chipmunks, Guinea Pigs, Hamsters, Mice, Muskrats, Porcupines, Prairie Dogs, Rats, Squirrels, Woodchucks

Lagomorphs
Hares, Pikas, Rabbits

Edentates
Anteaters, Armadillos, Sloths

Pangolins, or Scaly Anteaters

Aardvarks

Bats

Flying Lemurs

Primates
Apes, Lemurs, Man, Monkeys

STRANGE MAMMALS OF THE PAST

Baluchitherium, a giant hornless rhinoceros, lived in Asia 30 million years ago. This animal grew to be 17 feet tall and 27 feet long. It was the largest land mammal of all time, but it was by no means as large as the biggest dinosaurs.

Macrauchenia, which lived in South America during the Ice Age, looked much like a camel with the beginning of an elephant's trunk. It was not, however, closely related to either the camel or the elephant.

Synthetoceras, a deerlike mammal of North America, specialized in horns. In addition to two horns in the customary places and numerous bumps on its skull, this animal had a grotesquely long, forked horn just above its nostrils. **Synthetoceras** lived about five million years ago.

Uintatherium was a clumsy six-horned American mammal of 50 million years ago. It lived in the days of the little dawn horse, **Eohippus,** and in the same region. This beast was about the size of an elephant. It must have been quite stupid, for its brain was very small.

Platybelodon, the shovel-jawed mastodon, was an Asiatic mammal of some five million years ago. Its big lower jaw ending in two flat tusks made an excellent shovel for scooping up plant food.

Brontops was one of the "giant beasts," or titanotheres, of North America. It grew to be 8 feet high at the shoulders and 15 feet long. Its bowl-shaped skull left little room for brains. **Brontops** lived about 40 million years ago.

Andrewsarchus, a wolflike mammal of 50 million years ago, was the biggest meat-eating mammal that ever lived. Its skull was more than a yard long. This giant meat eater lived in Asia.

Ceratogaulus was a gopher of some 15 million years ago. Unlike any rodent of today, this ancient rodent had two horns. No one knows what purpose, if any, they served. The fossils of **Ceratogaulus** are found in North America.

Glyptodon was a giant armadillo of the Ice Age. In addition to its chief coat of armor, it had rings around its tail and a skullcap made of bony plates. This ancient armadillo lived in both North and South America.

MAMMAL FAMILIES

The several thousand kinds of mammals living today are grouped into 18 orders. These orders are divided into more than 100 families. This chart names eleven of the well-known mammal families and pictures some of the animals that belong in each.

BEAR (Ursidae)

SUN BEAR SPECTACLED BEAR SLOTH BEAR POLAR BEAR GRIZZLY BEAR BLACK BEAR (CINN

CAT (Felidae)

DOMESTIC CAT

BOBCAT

LEOPARD

COUGAR, OR PUMA, OR MOUNTAIN LION

OCELOT

LYNX

CHEETAH

JAGUAR

DEER (Cervidae)

VIRGINIA DEER

MOOSE

ELK, OR WAPITI

CARIBOU, OR REINDEER

WEASEL (Mustelidae)

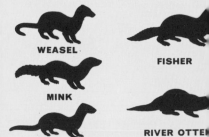
WEASEL

FISHER

MINK

RIVER OTTER

FERRET

MARTEN

SEA OTTER

CATTLE (Bovidae)

DAIRY COW

WATER BUFFALO

ZEBU

MOUNTAIN SHEEP

BISON

CHAMOIS

MOUNTAIN GOAT

DOMESTIC GOA

GNU

MUSKOX

YAK

DOMESTIC SHEEP

MOUSE (Cricetidae)

 DEER MOUSE

MEADOW MOUSE, OR VOLE

 HAMSTER

LEMMING

MUSKRAT

PACK RAT

SQUIRREL (Sciuridae)

CHIPMUNK

GOPHER

D SQUIRREL GRAY SQUIRREL FOX SQUIRREL

FLYING SQUIRREL

HOARY MARMOT

PRAIRIE DOG WOODCHUCK

TIGER

LION

DOG (Canidae)

DOMESTIC DOG

COYOTE

FOX

WOLF

CAMEL (Camelidae)

SKUNK

BADGER

WOLVERINE

VICUÑA

ARABIAN CAMEL

LLAMA

ALPACA

BACTRIAN CAMEL

GUANACO

APE (Simiidae, or Pongidae)

GIBBON

CHIMPANZEE

ORANGUTAN

GORILLA

HORSE (Equidae)

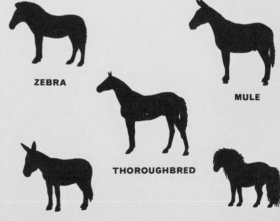
ZEBRA

MULE

THOROUGHBRED

DONKEY, OR ASS

SHETLAND PONY

DOGS

There are well over 100 breeds of dogs. At dog shows the many breeds are grouped into six main groups, or classes. The grouping does not mean that the dogs in a group are all closely related. Some are, but others may not be. This chart shows the six groups and some of the breeds in each.

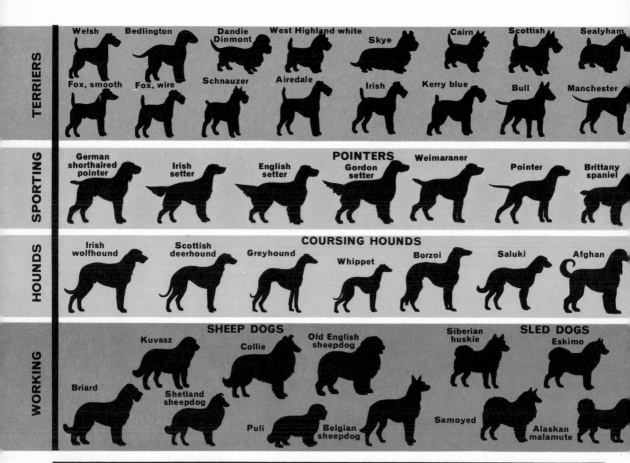

TERRIERS: Welsh, Bedlington, Dandie Dinmont, West Highland white, Skye, Cairn, Scottish, Sealyham, Fox, smooth, Fox, wire, Schnauzer, Airedale, Irish, Kerry blue, Bull, Manchester

SPORTING: German shorthaired pointer, Irish setter, English setter, POINTERS — Gordon setter, Weimaraner, Pointer, Brittany spaniel

HOUNDS: Irish wolfhound, Scottish deerhound, COURSING HOUNDS — Greyhound, Whippet, Borzoi, Saluki, Afghan

WORKING: Briard, Kuvasz, SHEEP DOGS — Collie, Shetland sheepdog, Old English sheepdog, Puli, Belgian sheepdog, Siberian huskie, SLED DOGS — Eskimo, Samoyed, Alaskan malamute

WINNERS IN MAJOR DOG SHOWS FROM 1950 TO 1962

	Westminster (New York)	Morris and Essex (Madison, N.J.)	International (Chicago)
1950	Ch. Walsing Winning Trick of Edgerstoune (Scottish terrier)	Ch. Tyronne Farm Clancy (Irish setter)	Ch. Walsing Winning Trick of Edgerstoune (Scottish terrier)
1951	Ch. Bang Away of Sirrah Crest (Boxer)	Ch. Rock Falls Colonel (English setter)	Ch. Foxbank Entertainer of Harham (Fox terrier, wire)
1952	Ch. Rancho Dobe's Storm (Doberman pinscher)	Ch. Wyretex Wyns Traveller of Trucote (Fox terrier, wire)	Ch. Edgerstoune Troubadour (Scottish terrier)
1953	Ch. Rancho Dobe's Storm (Doberman pinscher)	Ch. Toplight Template of Twin Ponds (Welsh terrier)	Ch. Jodo von Liebestraum (German shepherd dog)
1954	Ch. Carmor's Rise and Shine (Cocker spaniel)	No show	Ch. Ludar of Blue Bar (English setter)
1955	Ch. Kippax Fearnought (Bulldog)	Ch. Baroque of Quality Hill (Boxer)	Ch. Frejax Royalist (English springer spaniel)
1956	Ch. Wilber White Swan (Toy poodle)	Ch. Roadcoach Roadster (Dalmatian)	Ch. Barrage of Quality Hill (Boxer)
1957	Ch. Shirkan of Grandeur (Afghan)	Ch. Fircot L'Ballerine of Maryland (Miniature poodle)	Ch. Chik T'Sun of Caversham (Pekingese)
1958	Ch. Puttencove Promise (Standard poodle)	No show	Ch. Ben Dar's Winning Stride (English setter)
		Eastern (Boston)	
1959	Ch. Fontclair Festoon (Miniature poodle)	Ch. Merrybrook's Fair Reward (Fox terrier, wire)	Ch. Chik T'Sun of Caversham (Pekingese)
1960	Ch. Chik T'Sun of Caversham (Pekingese)	Ch. Bengal Sabu (Airedale)	Ch. Blanart Bewitching (Scottish terrier)
1961	Ch. Cappoquin Little Sister (Toy poodle)	Ch. Pixietown Serenade of Hadleigh (Pomeranian)	Ch. Conifer's Lance (Irish setter)
1962	Ch. Elfinbrook Simon (West Highland white terrier)	Ch. Gay Boy of Geddesburg (Beagle)	Ch. Gladjac Royal Oslo (Norwegian elkhound)

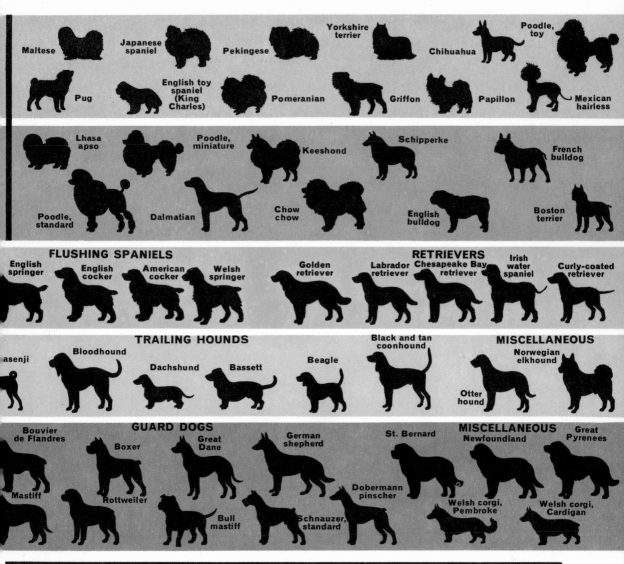

Maltese · Japanese spaniel · Pekingese · Yorkshire terrier · Chihuahua · Poodle, toy · Pug · English toy spaniel (King Charles) · Pomeranian · Griffon · Papillon · Mexican hairless

Lhasa apso · Poodle, miniature · Keeshond · Schipperke · French bulldog · Poodle, standard · Dalmatian · Chow chow · English bulldog · Boston terrier

FLUSHING SPANIELS — English springer · English cocker · American cocker · Welsh springer · **RETRIEVERS** — Golden retriever · Labrador retriever · Chesapeake Bay retriever · Irish water spaniel · Curly-coated retriever

TRAILING HOUNDS — Basenji · Bloodhound · Dachshund · Bassett · Beagle · Black and tan coonhound · **MISCELLANEOUS** — Norwegian elkhound · Otter hound

GUARD DOGS — Bouvier de Flandres · Boxer · Great Dane · German shepherd · St. Bernard · **MISCELLANEOUS** — Newfoundland · Great Pyrenees · Mastiff · Rottweiler · Bull mastiff · Schnauzer, standard · Dobermann pinscher · Welsh corgi, Pembroke · Welsh corgi, Cardigan

DOG POPULARITY

Year	English setter	Pointer	Collie	St. Bernard	Cocker spaniel	Boston terrier	Fox terrier	Beagle	Great Dane	Irish terrier	Airedale	Bulldog	Bull terrier	Pomeranian	French bulldog	German shepherd	Pekingese	Chow chow	Scottish terrier	Dachshund	Springer spaniel	Greyhound	Boxer	Chihuahua	Poodle
1900	1		2	3	4	5	6	7	8		9	10													
1910		7		1		9		2	10			3	4	5	6		8								
1920				4		2			9			1	7		6		8		3	5		10			
1930				10	7	1		3	6								9	2	5	4		8			
1940				10	1	3	5	2									7			4		6	8	9	
1950			4		1	6		2								10	9		8	5			3	7	
1955			7		3	9		1								6	10			5			2	4	8
1956			8		5	9		1								6	10			4			3	2	7
1957			8		7	10		1								6	9			3			4	2	5
1958			8		7	10		1								5	9			4			6	2	3
1959			9		6	10		1								5	8			4			7	3	2
1960			8		7	10		2								5	6			4			9	3	1
1961			7		8	9		2							10	5	6			3				4	1

ANIMAL RECORD HOLDERS

A pigmy goby is the smallest fish in the world and the smallest animal with a backbone. It is less than half an inch long.

The blue whale is the largest animal in the world. So far as anyone knows, it is the largest animal that ever lived. It may be more than 100 feet long and weigh more than 100 tons. It is a mammal.

The walking sticks are the longest of all insects. The longest are about 16 inches long.

The whale shark is the largest fish. It may be 45 feet long.

The anaconda is the longest and heaviest snake. It may be 37 feet long and weigh more than 250 pounds.

The Hercules moth of Australia has a wingspread of 14 inches and is the world's largest moth.

The African elephant is the largest land animal. It may weigh more than six tons. It is a mammal.

The true chameleon has the most amazing tongue found in the animal world. A seven-inch chameleon may have a twelve-inch tongue, which it can shoot out like lightning to catch an insect.

The giant tortoise is the longest-lived of all animals. It may live to be 150 years old.

The arctic tern takes the longest trips on its own power of any animal. An arctic tern may travel more than 20,000 miles in a single year.

FACTS ABOUT BRAINS

1 A full-grown person's brain weighs about 3½ pounds.

2 A gorilla's brain weighs about 1⅓ pounds.

3 An elephant has one pound of brain for every 1,000 pounds of body.

4 A blue whale weighs about 25 times as much as an elephant but its brain weighs only twice as much as an elephant's— about 20 pounds.

5 A dog's brain weighs about 6 ounces, a cat's about one ounce, and a horse's about 20 ounces.

6 The ordinary person weighs about 40 times as much as his brain.

7 A cod weighs about 5,000 times as much as its brain.

8 The brain of the 35-ton thunder lizard (*Brontosaurus*) weighed only about a pound. No wonder the dinosaurs disappeared from the earth!

9 The brain space in the skull of a person of today measures about 1,300 cubic centimeters. The brain space in the skull of the Java ape man (*Pithecanthropus erectus*) measured about 900 cubic centimeters.

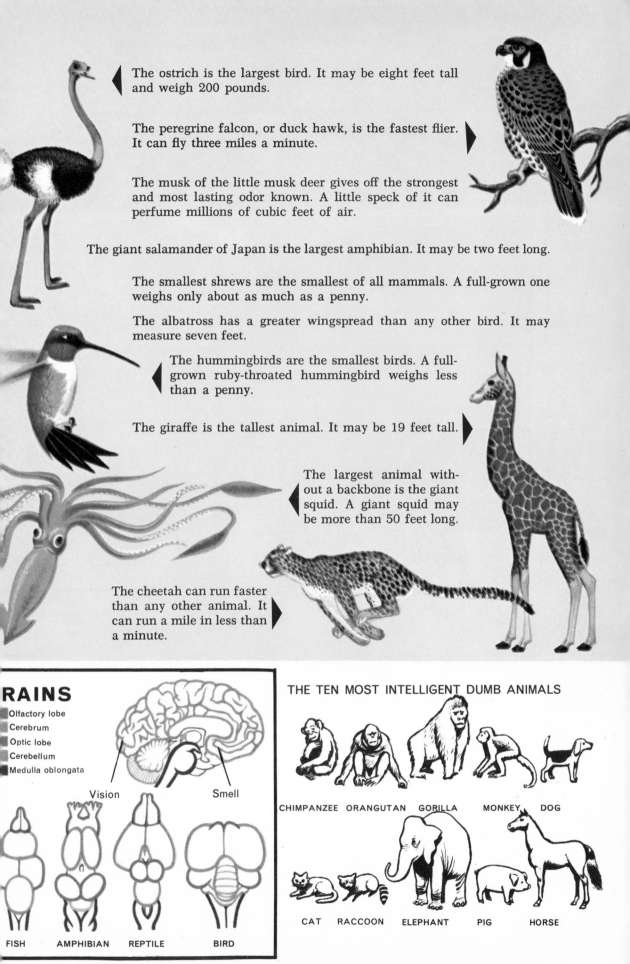

The ostrich is the largest bird. It may be eight feet tall and weigh 200 pounds.

The peregrine falcon, or duck hawk, is the fastest flier. It can fly three miles a minute.

The musk of the little musk deer gives off the strongest and most lasting odor known. A little speck of it can perfume millions of cubic feet of air.

The giant salamander of Japan is the largest amphibian. It may be two feet long.

The smallest shrews are the smallest of all mammals. A full-grown one weighs only about as much as a penny.

The albatross has a greater wingspread than any other bird. It may measure seven feet.

The hummingbirds are the smallest birds. A full-grown ruby-throated hummingbird weighs less than a penny.

The giraffe is the tallest animal. It may be 19 feet tall.

The largest animal without a backbone is the giant squid. A giant squid may be more than 50 feet long.

The cheetah can run faster than any other animal. It can run a mile in less than a minute.

RAINS

Olfactory lobe
Cerebrum
Optic lobe
Cerebellum
Medulla oblongata

Vision   Smell

FISH   AMPHIBIAN   REPTILE   BIRD

THE TEN MOST INTELLIGENT DUMB ANIMALS

CHIMPANZEE   ORANGUTAN   GORILLA   MONKEY   DOG

CAT   RACCOON   ELEPHANT   PIG   HORSE

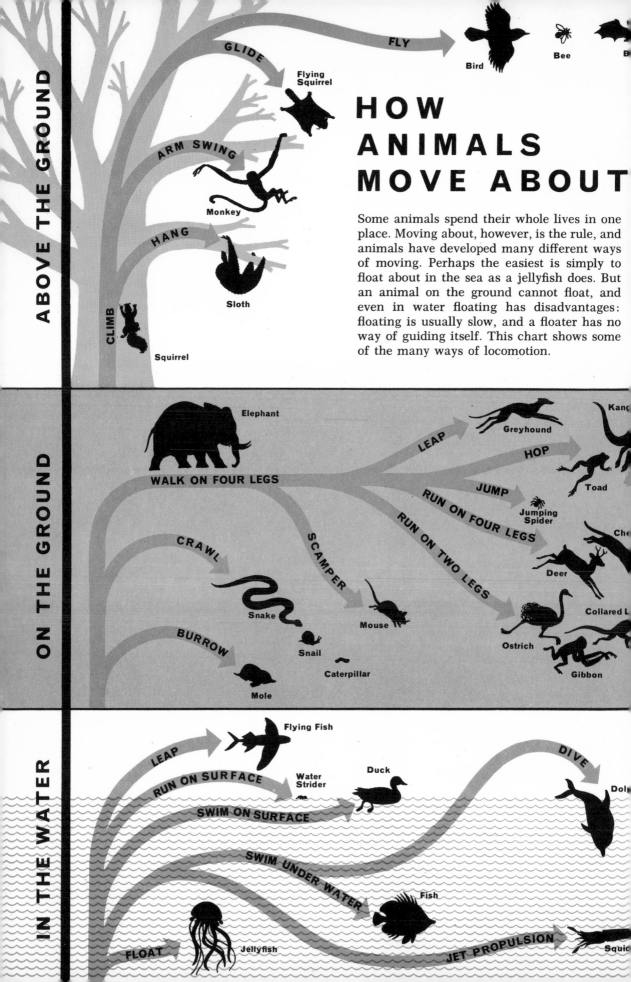

HOW ANIMALS MOVE ABOUT

Some animals spend their whole lives in one place. Moving about, however, is the rule, and animals have developed many different ways of moving. Perhaps the easiest is simply to float about in the sea as a jellyfish does. But an animal on the ground cannot float, and even in water floating has disadvantages: floating is usually slow, and a floater has no way of guiding itself. This chart shows some of the many ways of locomotion.

ABOVE THE GROUND

GLIDE — Flying Squirrel
FLY — Bird, Bee
ARM SWING — Monkey
HANG — Sloth
CLIMB — Squirrel

ON THE GROUND

Elephant
WALK ON FOUR LEGS
LEAP — Greyhound
HOP — Kang
JUMP — Jumping Spider
RUN ON FOUR LEGS — Toad
RUN ON TWO LEGS — Che
Deer
CRAWL — Snake
SCAMPER — Mouse
Snail
Caterpillar
BURROW — Mole
Ostrich
Collared L
Gibbon

IN THE WATER

LEAP — Flying Fish
RUN ON SURFACE — Water Strider
Duck
DIVE — Dol
SWIM ON SURFACE
SWIM UNDER WATER — Fish
FLOAT — Jellyfish
JET PROPULSION — Squid

DEER

AND WOLF **CAT**

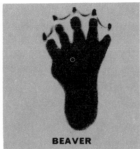
BEAVER

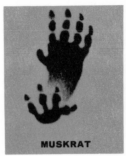
MUSKRAT

FOX

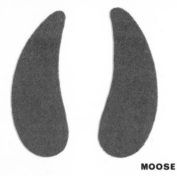
MOOSE

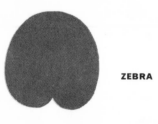
ZEBRA

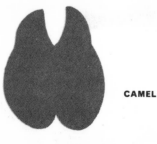
CAMEL

GIRAFFE

ANIMAL TRACKS

Animals leave trails as they move about in snow or in sand or mud. The feet of animals with legs make tracks; in some cases their tails do, too. A person who spends much time out of doors away from the city during the winter learns to know the tracks of many different animals. The pictures show the tracks of a few birds and mammals.

Some four-legged animals are "perfect" walkers. Their hind feet fit perfectly into the tracks made by their front feet. The cat is one; the fox is another.

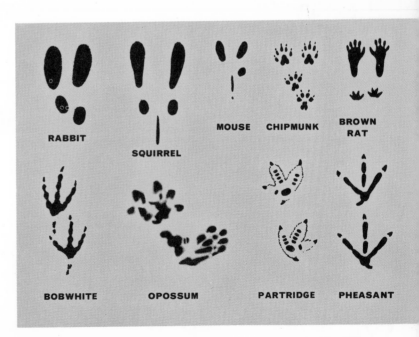

RABBIT SQUIRREL MOUSE CHIPMUNK BROWN RAT

BOBWHITE OPOSSUM PARTRIDGE PHEASANT

DID YOU KNOW?

Every termite nest has its king and queen. All the other termites in the nest—there may be millions—are their children.

Petrels get their name from Peter, one of the Twelve Apostles, who, according to the story in the New Testament, walked to Jesus on the waves of a storm-tossed lake. Petrels often hover close to the surface of the sea with their feet actually in the water and look as if they were walking on the waves.

Hummingbirds can fly backwards.

Some animals can grow, or regenerate, lost parts. A lobster that loses a claw can grow a new one. If a little flatworm is cut in two crossways, its head-half will grow a new tail, and its tail-half will grow a new head.

The duckbill, or platypus, is the only mammal that has poison glands.

Army ants, when they stop for a few days at a time on their marches, build nests out of their own bodies for their queen and for the larvas and pupas. When the stay is over, the ants forming the walls of a nest separate and are ready to march again.

Some crabs camouflage themselves by "planting" small animals such as sponges, sea anemones, and hedgehog hydroids on their backs. These animals stay where they are put.

Some kinds of ants and termites are farmers. They raise fungus gardens.

Ants and termites may have domesticated animals in their nests. These domesticated animals are other insects such as aphids, treehoppers, and beetles.

Seals, although they spend most of their lives in water, are always born on land and, as babies, have to be taught to swim.

The alligator is the only reptile with a loud voice. Its bellow can be heard a mile away.

The pika, or little chief hare, cuts hay during the summer, dries it in the sun, and stores it in cracks in rocks. In the winter the animal lives on food from its "hayloft."

A cricket can be used as a thermometer, because the number of times it chirps per minute varies with the temperature. At a temperature a little above freezing, it chirps 47 times a minute, and at 70° F., 150 times a minute.

TEN ANIMALS THAT HAVE BECOME EXTINCT IN MODERN TIMES

PASSENGER PIGEON
The last passenger pigeon anyone knows about died September 1, 1914, in a zoo in Cincinnati. A hundred and fifty years ago the passenger pigeon was so common in the United States that the size of the flocks was one of the wonders of the bird world. But much killing and the cutting down of the forests where the bird nested caused it to disappear.

ESKIMO CURLEW
In the fall Eskimo curlews used to fly southward from Newfoundland in such millions that they "darkened the sky." They were killed by the hundreds of thousands for food. Since 1900 no live birds have been seen.

WEST INDIAN SEAL
This seal was much hunted during colonial days and has not been seen at all since 1912.

QUAGGA
The quagga has been extinct since about 1880. It, too, was hunted so much that it could not survive. It was once very common on the grassy plains of Africa.

STELLER'S SEA COW
This sea cow was a relative of the manatee but was much larger. It was first discovered near Alaska about 1740 and was killed off in less than thirty years.

TREE SLOTH

MOLE

RAT

The tree sloth has four legs, but it never walks on them. Instead, it hangs by them from the branches of trees.

A mole 6 inches long has been known to dig a tunnel 100 yards long in a single night.

The water ouzel, a bird of the Rocky Mountains, often builds its nest back of a waterfall.

Paper wasps were making paper out of wood many thousands of years before people learned to do so.

The kiwi, a bird of New Zealand, has only small remnants of wings, which are completely hidden by feathers.

The Portuguese man-of-war is not a single animal but a whole colony of small animals.

A young bird may eat more than its weight in food in a single day.

A worker honeybee commits suicide by stinging an enemy, for it cannot pull out its sting. It tears its body to pieces trying to do so.

One pair of Norway rats could have 350 million descendants in only three years. There are, as a rule, ten litters a year with ten young in each litter.

A big sponge may furnish shelter for thousands of smaller animals. More than 17,000, among them some fishes, were counted in a sponge a yard across found near Florida.

In every flock of hens a peck order is established. Every hen except the lowest one in the peck order can peck certain hens, and every one except the one at the top can be pecked by others. The higher a hen is in the peck order, the better chances it has to get all the food it wants and a good roosting place.

Austria's famous white performing horses, the Lippizaners, are dark when they are colts. They do not get their white coats until they are at least three years old.

Honeybees tell their fellow workers by dances where nectar is to be found.

One of the most ingenious devices in nature is the silken door a trap-door spider builds to close the entrance to its nest.

Many people consider the Cape buffalo the most dangerous of all animals. More hunters have been killed by it than by any other big game animal.

GREAT AUK
The great auk has been extinct since about 1844. This bird, once very common on islands near the eastern coast of North America, was killed off by hunters who wanted its meat for food and its feathers for featherbeds.

HEATH HEN
In the early 1900's a big effort was made to save this game bird, which by that time was found only on Martha's Vineyard. It had been so common in colonial times that servants sometimes complained that they had to eat it too often. In spite of efforts to save it, it has disappeared.

CALIFORNIA GRIZZLY BEAR
There are not even any mounted specimens of this very big bear in museums. Early settlers in the West killed it because they were afraid of it.

DODO
The dodo once was common on two islands in the Indian Ocean. But it has been extinct since 1681. When the sailors who landed on the islands came near dodoes, the birds did not try to escape. They could not fly, but they did not even walk away. "As dumb as a dodo" came to be a common saying. Sailors, hogs, and monkeys killed the dodo off.

LABRADOR DUCK
The last known Labrador duck was killed near Long Island in 1875. No one knows very much about this bird—where it nested or exactly where it spent the winters. Probably hunters killed it chiefly for its feathers. At any rate, the only Labrador ducks of today are about forty stuffed specimens in museums.

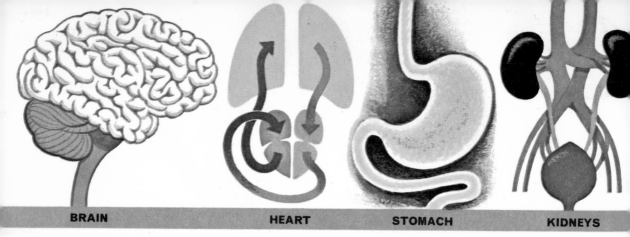

BRAIN   **HEART**   **STOMACH**   **KIDNEYS**

BODY SYSTEMS

SYSTEMS	PURPOSES SERVED	MADE UP OF
SKELETAL	Forms a framework for the body.	Bones and ligaments.
MUSCULAR	Brings about all body movements.	Muscles and tendons.
CIRCULATORY	Carries food and oxygen to all parts of the body and carries wastes away.	Heart, arteries, veins, capillaries, and blood.
DIGESTIVE	Digests food—turns it into a liquid—so that it can enter the blood, and gets rid of food wastes.	Mouth, teeth, throat, esophagus, stomach, liver, gallbladder, pancreas, small intestine, and large intestine.
RESPIRATORY	Takes in oxygen and gets rid of carbon dioxide.	Nose, throat, windpipe, bronchial tubes, and lungs.
NERVOUS	Acts as the body's engineer, lets a person know what is going on about him, and makes it possible to solve problems and to imagine.	Brain, spinal cord, and nerves.
ENDOCRINE	Produces hormones and by means of them controls some body activities.	Glands such as the pituitary, thyroid, parathyroids, adrenals, and islands of Langerhans.
URINARY	Removes wastes from blood and washes them from the body in urine.	Kidneys, ureters, bladder, and urethra.
LYMPHATIC	Keeps the cells of the body bathed in fluid, and passes food to the cells from the blood.	Lymph vessels, lymph glands, and lymph.
REPRODUCTIVE	Produces children.	Ovaries and uterus (female); testes (male).

IN ONE DAY

If an adult is of average weight and in good health, in every 24 hours:

His heart beats about 100,000 times.
His heart pumps about 3,000 gallons of blood.
He breathes about 23,000 times.
He breathes in about 400 cubic feet of air.
He takes out of the air about 20 cubic feet of oxygen.
He eats about 3 pounds of food.

He drinks about 3 pints of liquid.
He loses in perspiration about 1½ pints of water.
He turns in his sleep about 30 times.
His nails grow about .000046 of an inch.
His hair grows about .01714 of an inch.
He speaks about 5,000 words.

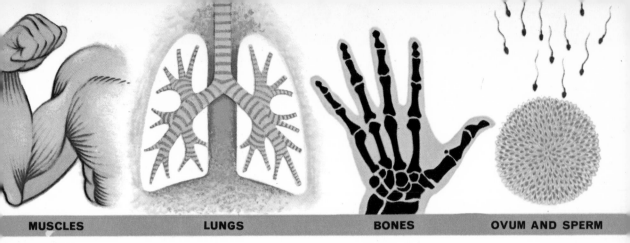

MUSCLES   LUNGS   BONES   OVUM AND SPERM

MORE FIGURES

The normal skeleton is made up of 206 bones; a child has more, but some of them fuse together as he grows up.

More than half of all a person's bones—106 to be exact—are in his wrists, ankles, hands, and feet.

At today's prices the value of the chemicals that make up a person's body is $1.17. The body contains ½ ounce of sugar, 1 ounce of salt, 3½ pounds of calcium, enough iron to make one nail, enough carbon for the leads of 9,000 pencils, enough phosphorus for the heads of 2,000 matches, and enough fat for 7 bars of soap.

A grown person's brain weighs about 3 pounds. The wrinkled, gray covering layer of the brain is made up of more than 9,000,-000,000 cells.

Messages travel along our nerves at speeds ranging from 1 foot to 300 feet a second.

There are more than 600 muscles in the muscular system.

A person has two sets of teeth. There are 20 teeth in the first, or baby, set; there are 32 in the second, or permanent, set.

Water accounts for about ⅔ of the weight of the body.

The stomach can be stretched to hold more than a quart.

A person's small intestine is from 3 to 4 times as long as he is tall. His large intestine is only 4 or 5 feet long.

The temperature marked "normal" on a fever thermometer is 98.6°F. The temperature of a healthy person is usually between 98°F. and 99°F. In a fever the temperature may rise to 110°F.

There are millions of tiny air sacs in the lungs. Their total inside surface is about 100 square yards.

A person normally breathes from 16 to 18 times a minute; the rate goes down during sleep and up during strenuous exercise.

The lungs can hold from 5 to 8 pints of air. About a pint is taken in at each breath.

A man's heart weighs 11 or 12 ounces, a woman's 8 or 9.

An adult weighing 150 pounds has about 6½ quarts of blood.

All the blood vessels of a person's body, if laid end to end, would reach 100,000 miles.

It takes a drop of blood only about one minute to leave the heart, circle the body, and get back to the heart again.

The normal pulse rate for an adult is from 60 to 80 beats a minute, with 70 the average while at rest.

In a person weighing 100 pounds there are about 20 trillion red blood cells and only 50 billion white cells.

Red blood cells live about 127 days. In a single day about 250 million are destroyed and replaced.

Red cells are so small that it would take thousands to make a pile 1 inch high.

The kidneys filter about 170 quarts of fluid a day to remove wastes. Most of the fluid they filter returns to the blood.

The complete skin covering of the body measures about 20 square feet.

In the skin of the palms of the hands there may be as many as 3,000 sweat glands to the square inch.

A person has from 90,000 to 140,000 hairs on his head. Red-haired people as a rule have fewer than brunettes or blondes.

SEEING

The eye is very much like a camera. It has a lens just as a camera has. The eye's lens is better than a camera lens because it can change its shape so as to focus the image of both far and near objects on the retina. The retina is like the film of the camera. The iris, which can change the size of the opening for light—the pupil—is like the diaphragm of the camera.

A person keeps his eyeball moist and clean by blinking. The average person blinks his eyes 25 times a minute. Each blink lasts about $\frac{1}{5}$ of a second.

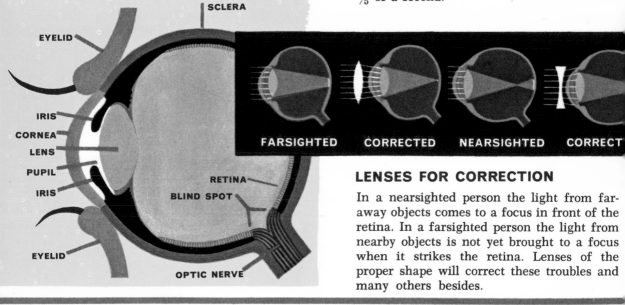

FARSIGHTED   CORRECTED   NEARSIGHTED   CORRECT

SCLERA · EYELID · IRIS · CORNEA · LENS · PUPIL · IRIS · RETINA · BLIND SPOT · EYELID · OPTIC NERVE

LENSES FOR CORRECTION

In a nearsighted person the light from far-away objects comes to a focus in front of the retina. In a farsighted person the light from nearby objects is not yet brought to a focus when it strikes the retina. Lenses of the proper shape will correct these troubles and many others besides.

HEARING

The nerves of hearing end in the cochlea of the inner ear. Sound waves strike the eardrum and make it vibrate. Little bones in the middle ear carry the vibrations to the liquid which fills the inner ear. The vibrations of this fluid affect the nerves that carry sound messages to the brain.

The semicircular canals which are a part of the inner ear are very important in helping a person keep his balance.

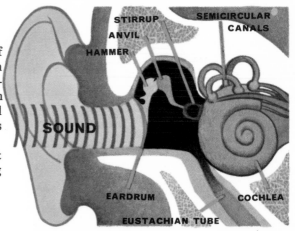

STIRRUP · ANVIL · HAMMER · SEMICIRCULAR CANALS · SOUND · EARDRUM · EUSTACHIAN TUBE · COCHLEA

FEELING

Different nerves of touch carry different messages, such as heat, cold, pain, touch, and pressure. In the skin alone there are 45 miles of nerves. Nerve endings are so close together in some areas of skin that pressure points with only $\frac{1}{25}$ of an inch between them can be told apart.

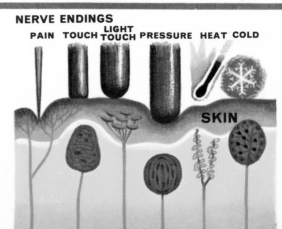

NERVE ENDINGS
PAIN · TOUCH · LIGHT TOUCH · PRESSURE · HEAT · COLD · SKIN

BLIND SPOT

On the retina of each eye there is a blind spot, the place where the tiny nerves of the retina unite to form the optic nerve. To show yourself that there is a blind spot, do this: Hold this page at arm's length. Close your left eye and look with your right eye at the cross below. You will be able to see the red dot, too. If you move the page toward you, the dot will disappear when the light reflected from it strikes the blind spot.

TEST FOR EYEDNESS

With both eyes open, point with your finger to some spot on the wall or ceiling of the room you are in. Close your right eye. Do not move your finger. Is your finger still pointing to the spot? Close your left eye. Is your finger still pointing to the spot? If your finger appears to have moved when you close your right eye, you are right-eyed. If your finger appears to have moved when you close your left eye, you are left-eyed.

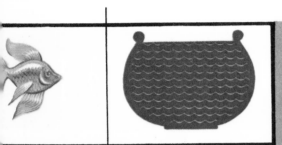

EYE BALANCE

Stand a 3 in. by 5 in. card on one of its longer edges on the line between the fishbowl and the fish. Bend down until your nose touches the card. One of your eyes now sees the fishbowl and the other the fish. Your brain will fuse the two pictures if your eyes have the proper balance, and you will see the fish in the bowl.

TASTING

In the tongue there are taste buds in which there are the endings of nerves of taste. There are buds of four kinds, giving us four taste sensations: sweet, sour, bitter, and salty. All other tastes are really smells. The sweet and salty taste buds are at the front of the tongue, the sour buds along the sides, and the bitter at the back. There are no taste buds in the middle of the tongue. A person has about 3000 taste buds. It takes a person about a third of a second to taste something salty and a whole second to taste something bitter.

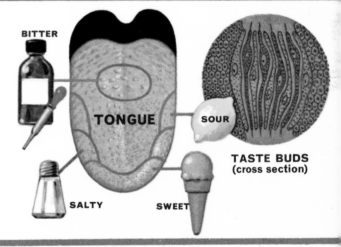

TASTE BUDS
(cross section)

SMELLING

All the endings of the nerves of smell are in the linings of the nose passages. Most of what we call taste is really smell. When one's nerves of smell are kept from doing their work by a cold, by dryness, or by some permanent injury, most foods taste alike.

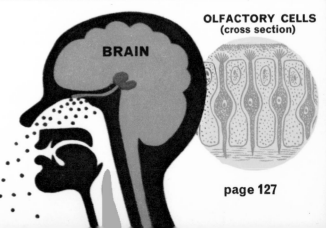

OLFACTORY CELLS
(cross section)

THE CHANGE IN U.S. DEATH RATES FROM DISEASES IN THIS CENTURY

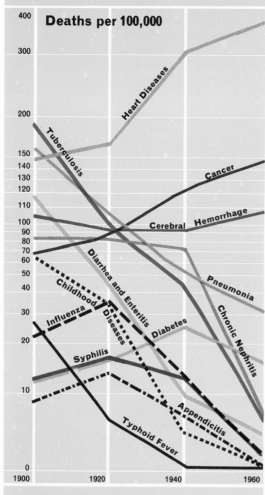

Deaths per 100,000

400
300
200
150
140
130
120
110
100
90
80
70
60
50
40
30
20
10
0

Heart Diseases

Tuberculosis

Cancer

Cerebral Hemorrhage

Diarrhea and Enteritis

Childhood Diseases

Influenza

Pneumonia

Chronic Nephritis

Diabetes

Syphilis

Appendicitis

Typhoid Fever

1900   1920   1940   1960

CHILDHOOD DISEASES

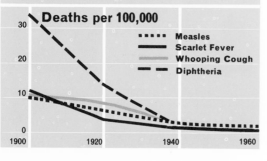

Deaths per 100,000

30

20

10

0

...... Measles
——— Scarlet Fever
——— Whooping Cough
– – – Diphtheria

1900   1920   1940   1960

DISEASE

TERMS TO UNDERSTAND

Acquired Immunity to a disease comes from having had an attack of the disease or from having been vaccinated against it.

Antibiotics are drugs produced by small organisms such as molds and soil bacteria. Among the antibiotics are penicillin, streptomycin, chloromycetin, aureomycin, tetracycline, terramycin, erythromycin, magamycin, polymyxin, tyrothrycin, and bacitracin.

Antibodies are substances which are produced in the bodies of animals and which counteract the effects of toxins and other substances produced in diseases.

Antigens are the toxins and similar substances which antibodies work against.

Antiseptics are substances which destroy disease germs.

Antitoxins are antibodies that counteract the effects of toxins produced by disease germs. Antitoxins of various diseases are obtained from animals into whose bodies the toxins of those diseases have been introduced. The antitoxins can then be injected into persons ill with those diseases.

Antivenins are antitoxic substances that counteract the poisons injected by snakebite.

Carriers are persons who have recovered from an attack of some infectious disease but who still have the germs of the disease in their bodies and can pass them on to others.

Chronic Diseases are long-lasting, not acute, diseases. Arthritis is a chronic disease.

Contagious Diseases are diseases which are passed directly or indirectly from one person to another. The word "contagious" comes from "contact."

Epidemics are widespread outbreaks of infectious diseases.

Gamma Globulin comes from blood plasma and is rich in antibodies. It is used in fighting measles.

Immunity to a disease means security against an attack of that disease.

DISEASE GERMS	BACILLI	COCCI	SPIROCHETES	RICKETTSIAE	VIRUSES	PROTOZO
page 128	Tuberculosis Diphtheria Typhoid fever Tetanus Whooping cough Plague Tularemia	Pneumonia Scarlet fever Erysipelas Meningitis	Syphilis Relapsing fever	Rocky Mountain spotted fever Typhus Q fever of Australia Tsutsugamushi	Mumps Measles Influenza Smallpox Yellow fever Common cold Chicken pox Poliomyelitis Hydrophobia	Malaria Amebic dyse African sleep sickness

Infectious Diseases are diseases caused by disease germs. An infectious disease may or may not be contagious.

Inoculation is commonly the injection of weakened germs into a person's body so that he will have the disease mildly and become immune to it. It may also mean the injection of serums, gamma globulin, or toxins.

Natural Immunity to a disease is the immunity which a person may have to the disease when he is born.

Pandemics are very widespread epidemics.

Plasma is the fluid portion of the blood—the blood, that is, minus the red and the white cells and the platelets.

Serums are clear liquids which are obtained from animals, usually from their blood, and which contain antibodies the animals have produced after germs or their toxins have been injected into them.

Toxins are poisons produced by disease germs.

Vaccines are germ or toxin preparations which bring about acquired immunity to a disease by stimulating the production of antibodies. Smallpox vaccine is lymph, usually taken from a cow, which contains weakened germs of smallpox.

Vectors are animal carriers of disease germs.

TESTS

The *Dick test* determines whether a person is immune to scarlet fever. A small amount of scarlet fever toxin is injected under the skin. If the person being tested is not immune, red spots will appear on the skin after 24 hours.

The *Schick test* determines whether a person is immune to diphtheria. A small amount of diphtheria toxin is injected under the skin. If the area becomes inflamed, the person being tested is not immune.

The *tuberculin test* determines whether the person being tested is or has ever been infected with tuberculosis. A small dose of tuberculin is injected into the skin. The test is called positive if there is a reddening of the skin in the area within a few hours. Most people have been infected and therefore give a positive test by the time they have finished high school, but in a high percentage of cases the disease has been overcome.

EPIDEMICS AND THE CONQUEST OF DISEASE THROUGH THE CENTURIES

5th B.C.	Plague in Athens
A.D. 3rd	Plague in Rome
Average Expectation of Life—22 Years	
4th	First hospital–St. Basil's at Caesarea
6th	Epidemic smallpox in France
12th	"Most dire famine, pestilence, and murrain in all England"–Anglo-Saxon Chronicle
14th	The Black Death
16th	Pandemic influenza Epidemic diphtheria in Amsterdam and the Rhineland Black assizes (jail fever, or typhus) of Cambridge
Average Expectation of Life—35 Years	
17th	Yellow fever at Guadaloupe Epidemic typhoid fever in England Great plague of London Pandemic malaria in Europe Treatment of malaria by cinchona bark (quinine)
18th	Spread of diphtheria to America Vaccine for smallpox
19th	Pandemic cholera Pandemic influenza Whooping cough a leading cause of infant mortality in England Germ theory of communicable disease Antiseptic surgery Pasteur treatment for hydrophobia Vaccine against typhoid Diphtheria antitoxin
Average Expectation of Life—45 Years	
20th	Plague in India–10,000,000 dead between 1900 and 1920 Pandemic influenza Reed's experiments with yellow fever Insulin for treatment of diabetes Antitoxin for scarlet fever, tetanus, and various childhood diseases Vaccine for poliomyelitis DDT for killing insect carriers of typhus, plague, and malaria Sulfa drugs Penicillin, streptomycin, and other "miracle drugs"
Average Expectation of Life—70 Years	

ANIMAL CARRIERS OF DISEASE	HOUSEFLY	FLEA	TICK	MOSQUITO	LOUSE	TSETSE FLY
	Typhoid fever Dysentery	Bubonic plague Typhus	Rocky Mountain spotted fever Tularemia	Yellow fever Malaria	Typhus Parrot fever	Sleeping sickness

LIGHT: TERMS TO UNDERSTAND

The unit for measuring the intensity of the light given off by a luminous object is the *candlepower*. A 60-candlepower lamp produces as much light as 60 candles of a standard size.

Light produced without noticeable heat is called *cold light*. The light fireflies flash is a good example.

The *complementary color* of any color is the color which, combined in the right proportion with the given color, produces white.

A *concave* surface is one curved inward to the center. A *convex* surface is one curved outward to the center.

When rays of light are scattered, we say that they are *diffused*.

Anything hot enough to give off light is said to be *incandescent*.

Light of different colors differs in wave length. The longest waves we can see are red waves; the shortest are violet. *Infrared rays* are somewhat longer than red rays. We cannot see them, but we can use them for taking pictures.

Luminous objects are those which give off light of their own.

A concave or convex piece of glass or some other transparent material used to make rays of light passing through them either come together or spread out is called a *lens*.

A *mirage* is a kind of optical illusion. Travelers in deserts, for example, see water ahead when there is no water there.

Anything which can be seen only by reflected light is said to be *nonluminous*.

A given piece or amount of material is called *opaque* if it allows no light to go through it.

An *optical illusion* is a mistaken picture our eyes give us.

A *prism* is a wedge-shaped piece of some transparent material such as glass by means of which light can be bent.

The bending back of light rays from a surface they strike is called *reflection*.

The bending of light rays as they travel at a slant from one transparent substance to another is called *refraction*.

A *translucent* substance is one which allows light rays to pass through but which scatters them and thus cannot be seen through clearly.

A *transparent* substance is one which allows light rays to pass through without scattering them and thus can be seen through clearly.

Ultraviolet rays are shorter than violet rays and cannot, therefore, be seen by the human eye. They are, however, useful, and special lamps are made to send them out.

REFLECTED REFLECTIONS

AN EXPERIMENT

Stand a pin straight up in a piece of cardboard. Lay two flat mirrors on the cardboard, one at each side of the pin. Tilt both mirrors slowly toward the pin. You will see more and more reflections of the pin in the mirrors until you have a "pinwheel." Remove one mirror and, no matter how much you tilt the remaining mirror, there will be only one reflection.

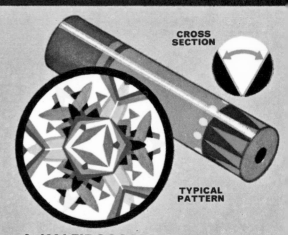

CROSS SECTION

TYPICAL PATTERN

A KALEIDOSCOPE

In a kaleidoscope there is an object box at one end into which scraps of colored glass or plastic are put. The reflections of these colored bits of material back and forth between the two mirrors make an interesting pattern. The pattern changes when the bits of material change position.

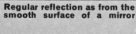
Mirror Writing

This mirror writing shows clearly that a mirror picture is reversed. In a mirror a person's left eye appears to be his right eye, and so on.

TWO WAYS OF SEEING THROUGH A BOOK

(TUBE OF DARK PAPER OR CARDBOARD)

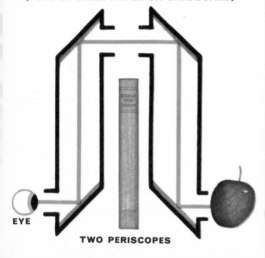

EYE

TWO PERISCOPES

KINDS OF REFLECTION

Regular reflection as from the smooth surface of a mirror

Diffused reflection as from the rough surface of woolen cloth

COOKIE CUPCAKE

Stand a mirror on edge along the red line. Try to read the words in the mirror. Why is one easier to read than the other?

BOX HIDE

Read these words by standing a mirror on edge on the red line.

Copy this pattern of dots on a big sheet of white paper. Lay the paper on a flat surface in front of a mirror. By looking in the mirror, not at the paper, try to join the dots to make the picture of a boat with a sail.

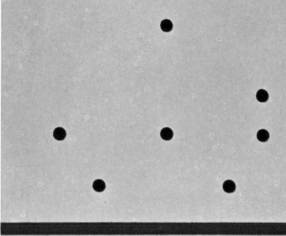

IMPORTANT USES OF MIRRORS

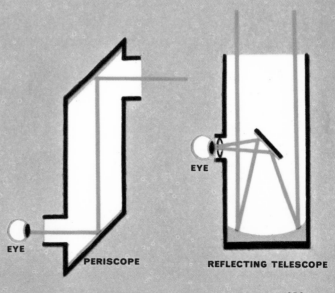

EYE

EYE

PERISCOPE

REFLECTING TELESCOPE

OPTICAL ILLUSIONS

These letters can be read almost as readily as if they were fully drawn.

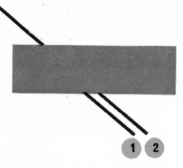

Is the line above the rectangle a continuation of 1 or 2?

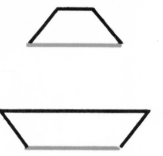

The red lines in these two figures are the same length.

This hat is no taller than it is wide.

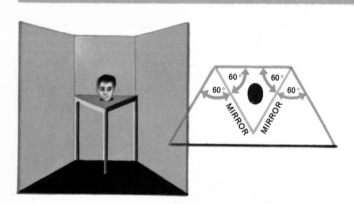

A SIMPLE MAGICIAN'S TRICK

In this trick a head appears to have no body. The optical illusion is brought about with mirrors. As a result of having the walls and mirrors at exactly the right angles, the walls and floor reflected in the mirrors appear to be the wall back of the table and the floor under it. Actually the man's body is hidden by the mirrors.

MOVING PICTURES

Divide two 3 in. by 5 in. cards in half as shown in the illustration. On the upper half of one draw a copper flower bowl. On the upper half of the second card draw an outline of the same bowl very lightly in pencil. Then draw bright-colored flowers to fill it. Now erase the pencil outline; it is meant only to help you place the flowers correctly.

Turn one of the cards upside down. Put the two cards back to back and fasten them with a rubber band to a straight rod or pencil. Hold the rod or pencil by the ends and twirl the cards. You should see the flowers in the bowl. Your eyes hold any picture they see for a short time. When the cards are twirled fast, your eyes see both pictures at the same time.

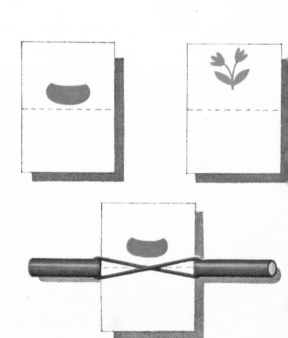

The two frames are perfect squares.

The two center circles have exactly the same diameter.

The center rectangles are equally dark.

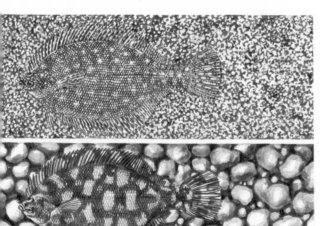

CAMOUFLAGE

Colors and color patterns help to protect many animals. Some animals change colors when their surroundings change.

During the World Wars much was done with color and color patterns to camouflage troops, warships, airplanes, tanks, and military installations of various kinds. By the end of World War II, however, infrared photographs taken from airplanes were "seeing through" camouflage paint and making camouflage much more difficult.

LENSES

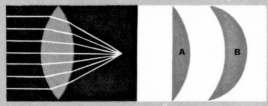

The lens in the first picture is a double convex lens. It brings rays of light to a focus. The two lenses in the second picture are convex lenses, too. They also make rays of light come together, or converge.

The lens in the third picture is a double concave lens. It spreads rays of light farther apart. The lenses in the last picture are concave lenses, too. They can both be used to make rays of light spread apart, or diverge.

TWO EXPERIMENTS WITH REFRACTION

Put a small, shallow metal or opaque plastic bowl on a table. Place a coin on the bottom of the bowl. Move the bowl away from you slowly until the far edge of the coin is just out of sight. Then have someone pour water into the bowl. The coin will come into view.

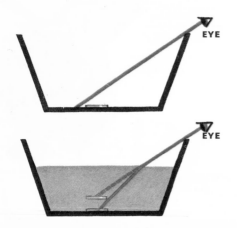

The light reflected from the coin is bent as it goes at a slant from the water into the air. When the coin comes into view after water has been poured into the bowl you are seeing it not where it really is but in the direction from which the light enters your eye.

Stand a pencil in a tumbler two-thirds full of water so that it rests against the top edge. The bending of the rays of light as they pass through the water into the air not only makes the pencil appear to be broken at the surface of the water but also makes the part in the water appear to be bigger around than it is. The curve of the side of the tumbler makes the water a magnifying "glass."

IMPORTANT USES OF LENSES

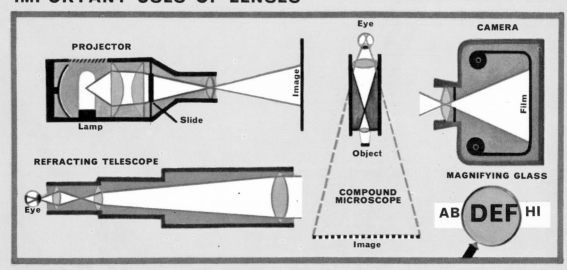

THE SPECTRUM

With a prism sunlight can be broken up into the colors of which it is made. The colors are violet, indigo, blue, green, yellow, orange, and red.

DOUBLE RAINBOW

A rainbow is formed when droplets of water in the air act as prisms. Sometimes there is a double rainbow. In the two rainbows of a double rainbow the colors, as the diagram shows, are reversed.

WHY A RED ROSE IS RED

The petals of a red rose absorb all the colors except red. They reflect the red rays to our eyes, and the rose therefore looks red.

A DISAPPEARING CAGE

Lay a piece of bright-red cellophane over this picture. The cage disappears, and the parrot is free to fly away.

The red cellophane allows only red and orange rays to pass through it. The red-orange rays from the cage are lost in the red-orange rays reflected from the white background. The cage therefore disappears. At the same time, since no blue rays or green rays can go through the cellophane, the parrot is now all red and black.

AFTERIMAGE

Stare at the red birds while you count to 30. Then look up quickly to the ceiling of the room you are in. You should see blue-green birds there. If the ceiling is too dark for the birds to show, look at a sheet of white paper instead.

When you stare at the birds your eyes become too tired of red to see it any longer. When you look at the ceiling you still see the birds for a very short time, but you see them as blue-green. If the birds in the picture were blue, you would see them as brownish-yellow when you looked up at the ceiling.

LAMPS AND LIGHTING

BURNING BRAND   **GREEK**   **ROMAN**

TORCHES

Fires lighted up the caves of our caveman ancestors. Some prehistoric man discovered that he could get a light to carry with him by taking a burning brand from his fire. Ancient Greek torches were made of bronze; they held oil-soaked rags in the hollowed-out ends. Roman torches were bundles of oil-soaked sticks fastened to long poles.

PAUL REVERE CANDLE LANTERN

PRICKET CHANDELIER

CANDLESTICK

CANDLES

No one knows who first discovered how to make a candle by dipping a cord, or wick, time after time in melted tallow. We do know, however, that candlemaking was very common in the monasteries of the Middle Ages. And candlemaking was one of the skills the Colonists brought to the New World. Candles are still popular. Most of today's candles are made of paraffin.

ROMAN   **BETTY LAMP**   **KEROSENE LAMP**

OIL LAMPS

It would be easy to fill a whole book with pictures of oil lamps. They have been used for more than two thousand years. Fish oil, whale oil, and kerosene are among the oils that have been burned in them. The lamp chimney greatly improved kerosene lamps. The flame burns much more steadily with the steady upward flow of air the chimney provides.

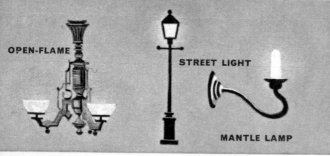

OPEN-FLAME   **STREET LIGHT**   **MANTLE LAMP**

GAS LAMPS

For a time in the 1800's gas lamps were very popular. Both natural gas and gas manufactured from coal were used. At first all gas lamps had open flames. Then the gas mantle was invented. It consists of a hood for the flame made of a thin sheet of a mixture of materials which will not burn but which does become white-hot and incandescent.

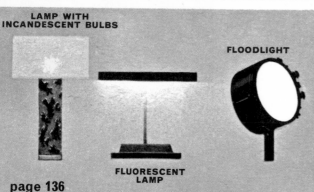

LAMP WITH INCANDESCENT BULBS

FLOODLIGHT

FLUORESCENT LAMP

ELECTRIC LAMPS

Electric lamps are very different from all the kinds of lamps that went before them: in them nothing burns. Different kinds of electric lamps work in different ways. In those most of us know best, a filament is made incandescent by the flowing of electricity through it. No electric lamps of any kind could be had until 1878, when the first arc lamp was made. Today they have largely replaced other kinds of lamps and lighting.

GREAT LIGHTHOUSES

For many centuries lighthouses have warned sailors of dangerous places along seacoasts. The most famous lighthouse of ancient times was the Pharos of Alexandria—one of the Seven Wonders of the Ancient World.

The first lighthouse built in the United States after the Colonies won their independence was built on Cape Henry, Virginia. Fish oil was first used for its lamps, then whale oil, lard oil, kerosene, gas, and finally electricity. The oldest lighthouse on the Pacific coast of the United States was built in 1860 on Point Loma in California.

The highest lighthouse in the United States is at Lehua, Hawaii. It is 709 feet above sea level. The highest in the west coast states is on Santa Rosa Island, California. It is 530 feet above sea level. The highest lighthouse on the Atlantic coast of the United States— 278 feet above sea level—is on Marcus Hook, Delaware.

Among the famous European lighthouses are Eddystone in the English Channel, Fastnet Rock off the coast of Ireland, Bishop Rock off the coast of Scotland, and Vierge Tower on the French coast.

The Oak Island lighthouse on the North Carolina coast can send out beams of 14,000,000 candlepower. That at Molokai, Hawaii, rates 12,000,000 in candlepower. Other American lighthouses of more than 1,000,000 candlepower are:

Brazos River, Tex.	Hillsboro Inlet, Fla.
Buzzard's Bay, Mass.	Kilauea Point, Hawaii
Cape Charles, Va.	Liston Range, Del.
Cape Kumuhaki, Hawaii	Nawiliwili, Hawaii
Cape May, N. J.	Pensacola, Fla.
Cape St. Elias, Alaska	Point Arena, Cal.
Cape San Juan, P. R.	Point Arguello, Cal.
Cape Spencer, Alaska	Point Borinquen, P. R.
Cubits Gap, La.	Rawley Point, Mich.
Dry Tortugas, Fla.	Rock of Ages, Mich.
Fire Island, N. Y.	Santa Barbara, Cal.
Harbor of Refuge, Del.	White Shoal, Mich.

LIVING LANTERNS

Most of the living things around us we see only by reflected light. But some living things give off light of their own.

Fireflies are probably the best known of all living lanterns. A firefly has a light organ on its abdomen. It can turn its light off and on.

Of the other animal lanterns, some glow all over; others have definite light organs. Some glow continually; others are like the firefly in flashing on their lights only at times.

Animals are not very common in the deep sea, but about two-thirds of those that are there are luminous. Some of them send out into the water a material which forms a luminous cloud. Although the deep sea gets no sunlight at all, it is not entirely dark.

Not all living lanterns are animals. The jack-o'-lantern is one of the several mushrooms that shine in the dark. A number of kinds of bacteria are luminous. These bacteria often make decaying meat shine. Some animals, moreover, are luminous because they have luminous bacteria in their bodies. One fish, for example, has little tubes near its eyes in which there are many luminous bacteria.

Luminous bacteria are probably the smallest of living lanterns. A single bacterium does not give off enough light for our eyes to see, but millions together shine very noticeably.

LUMINOUS SHRIMP

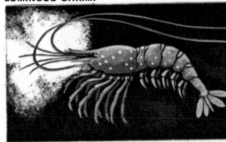

HATCHETFISH

JACK-O'-LANTERN MUSHROOM

Great Pyramid

Colossus of Rhodes

Statue of Zeus

Hanging Gardens of Babylon

Temple of Diana at Ephesus

Mausoleum at Halicarnassus

Pharos of Alexandria

THE SEVEN WONDERS
OF THE ANCIENT WORLD

Even in ancient times men built many remarkable structures. Seven were so wonderful that they came to be called the Seven Wonders of the World. One of the Seven Wonders is still standing—the Great Pyramid.

Strangely enough, the *Great Pyramid* was built long before any other of the Seven Wonders—more than 4,500 years ago. Planned by King Khufu of Egypt as a tomb for himself, it stands not far from the modern city of Cairo. More than 2 million blocks of stone, each weighing about three tons, were used in this great structure. When finished it rose to 481 feet and had a base 755 feet square.

The *Hanging Gardens of Babylon* were built by Nebuchadnezzar, the king of Babylon, about 2,500 years ago. These gardens were on the tops of towering walls that surrounded the king's palace. The walls themselves were as remarkable as the gardens. The highest rose some 300 feet. They all crumbled away long ago; we know about them only from ancient writings.

The *Statue of Zeus* at Olympia in Greece has been called the most wonderful statue ever made. It was the work of the famous Greek sculptor Phidias and dates back about 2,400 years. In the beliefs of the ancient Greeks Zeus was the king of the gods. This statue of him was covered with gold and ivory and had jewels for eyes. No traces of it remain.

The *Temple of Diana at Ephesus,* in Asia Minor, also dates back about 2,400 years. This temple, built to honor the Greek goddess of the moon and of hunting, was famous for the beauty of its huge pillars. They were some 60 feet tall. The temple was destroyed by invaders after it had stood for about 600 years. In its heyday so many gifts were brought to the temple by worshipers of Diana that it was a great treasure house.

The *Mausoleum at Halicarnassus,* in Asia Minor, was the tomb of Mausolus, a king who died in 353 B.C. It was supposedly the most beautiful tomb of ancient times. It rose for 100 feet and was surmounted by a magnificent statue of a chariot drawn by prancing horses. In the chariot were the figures of Mausolus and his queen. After standing for 19 centuries, the mausoleum was destroyed by an earthquake. There are some remnants of it in the British Museum.

The great statue called the *Colossus of Rhodes* was built about 22½ centuries ago to celebrate a victory by the people of Rhodes, one of the states of ancient Greece. It was a statue of the god Apollo. The statue was made of bronze and was some 100 feet tall—about two-thirds as tall as the Statue of Liberty. It stood at the entrance to the harbor of Rhodes. Only 56 years after it was finished, an earthquake destroyed it.

The *Pharos of Alexandria,* built about 22 centuries ago, was a lighthouse which for more than 1,500 years guarded the harbor of Alexandria in Egypt. The lighthouse was a stone tower about 400 feet tall, at the top of which bonfires were kept burning. Ideas differ as to how it was destroyed. Some records say that an earthquake destroyed it. Others say that Arabs destroyed it thinking that it was full of treasure.

SEVEN WONDERS
OF THE MODERN WORLD

Jodrell Bank Telescope

Hoover Dam

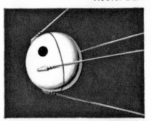
Sputnik I

Panama Canal

Golden Gate Bridge

Empire State Building

Nautilus

It is hard to pick out *the* seven wonders of the modern world—there are a very great many to choose from. The seven structures pictured below are certainly wonders, even if some people consider other things man has built in modern times even more remarkable.

The *Empire State Building* in New York City is the world's tallest skyscraper. The top of this 102-story building is nearly a quarter of a mile above street level. The "Empire State" contains enough floor space for a city of 80,000 people. It has seven miles of elevator shafts. The wires carrying the current for its lights, motors, telephones, and other electric devices would, if joined end to end, reach nearly twice around the earth at the equator.

The *Jodrell Bank Telescope* is in England. Its curved reflecting surface is 250 feet across. This great instrument is a radio, not an optical, telescope. It receives radio signals sent out by stars and other heavenly bodies. With its help, heavenly bodies about which astronomers knew nothing at all earlier have been located. It can "hear" billions of light-years out into space through earth clouds and clouds of star dust. Its success led to the building of even larger radio telescopes.

The *Golden Gate Bridge,* which joins the city of San Francisco with the opposite side of the Golden Gate, has as its chief part the longest single suspension span in the world. This span is 4,200 feet long. The tops of the towers that support the weight of the span are 750 feet above the water; the foundations reach down to bedrock. The main cables are 36½ inches in diameter. Each cable is 7,650 feet long and is made of thousands of wires. It took 80,000 miles of wire for the two.

The *Panama Canal* has been called jokingly the "world's biggest ditch." This canal cuts through the narrow neck of land joining North America with South America—the Isthmus of Panama. The canal is 50 miles long, 300 feet wide, and 41 feet deep. It has 12 locks. For a part of the way the canal had to be driven through solid rock. More than 200 million tons of rock and soil were removed.

Sputnik I was the first artificial moon, or satellite. The Russians launched it by means of a very powerful rocket. This satellite weighed 23 pounds. It traveled around the earth hundreds of times, making each trip in a little more than 96 minutes. When it finally fell to the earth, it was burned up in the earth's atmosphere. Its success started people to thinking seriously of space travel.

The *Hoover Dam* across the Colorado River on the border line between Nevada and Arizona is not the world's biggest or longest dam, but it ranks at the top of the world's great dams when both its height and the size of the artificial lake it helps form are taken into account. The dam is 726 feet tall and 1,244 feet long; its concrete base is 660 feet thick. Lake Mead, its reservoir, is 247 square miles in area and holds nearly 10,000 billion gallons of water.

The *Nautilus,* one of the ships of the United States Navy, was the first submarine to be driven by atomic power. This submarine made a name for itself in August of 1958 by traveling under the ice across the North Pole.

THIRTY UNITED STATES MISSILES

ICBM=Intercontinental ballistic missile
IRBM=Intermediate range ballistic missile

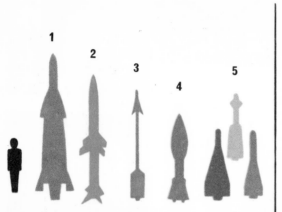
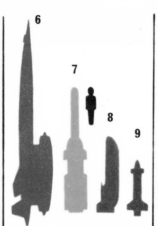

AIR TO AIR
1 Eagle
2 Sparrow
3 Sidewinder
4 Genie
5 Falcon

AIR TO GROUND
6 Hound Dog
7 Skybolt
8 Quail
9 Bullpup

SUBMARINE TO LAND SURFACE
10 Polaris (IRBM)

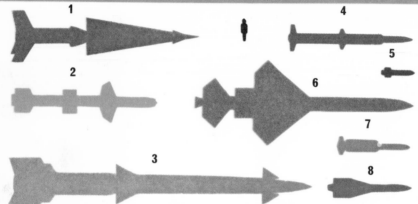

SURFACE OF LAND OR SEA TO AIR
1 Nike Hercules
2 Talos
3 Nike Zeus
4 Terrier
5 Mauler
6 Bomarc
7 Tartar
8 Hawk

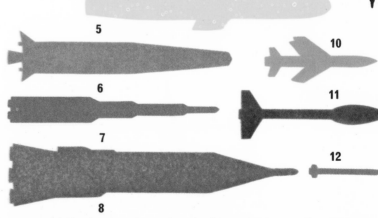

GROUND TO GROUND
1 Jupiter (IRBM)
2 Redstone
3 Sergeant
4 Mace
5 Thor (IRBM)
6 Minuteman (ICBM)
7 Atlas (ICBM)
8 Titan (ICBM)
9 Pershing
10 Lacrosse
11 Honest John
12 Little John

IMPORTANT UNMANNED FLIGHTS OF THE EARLY SPACE AGE

EARTH SATELLITES

Name	Nation	Date of Launching	Life or Life Expectancy	Weight of Satellite	Farthest Point of Orbit (Apogee)	Nearest Point of Orbit (Perigee)	Time Needed for One Revolution Around Earth	Additional Information
Sputnik I	U.S.S.R.	Oct. 4, 1957	3 mos. Fell Jan. 4, 1958	183.6 lbs.	588 mi.	142 mi.	96.2 min.	Measured temperature and pressure aloft.
Sputnik II	U.S.S.R.	Nov. 3, 1957	6 mos. Fell Apr. 14, 1958	1120 lbs.	1038 mi.	140 mi.	103.7 min.	Carried a little dog, Laika, aloft.
Explorer I	U.S.A.	Jan. 31, 1958	5-7 years	18.13 lbs.	1573 mi.	224 mi.	114.8 min.	Discovered a belt of dangerous radiation surrounding earth.
Vanguard I	U.S.A.	Mar. 17, 1958	1000 years	3.25 lbs.	2466 mi.	404 mi.	133.9 min.	Helped show earth is slightly pear-shaped.
Score-Atlas	U.S.A.	Dec. 18, 1958	35 days. Fell Jan. 21, 1959	150 lbs.	920 mi.	110 mi.	101.5 min.	Broadcast a Christmas message from President Eisenhower.
Discoverer I	U.S.A.	Feb. 28, 1959	5 days. Fell Mar. 5, 1959	245 lbs.	605 mi.	99 mi.	95.9 min.	First satellite in a polar orbit.
Explorer VI	U.S.A.	Aug. 7, 1959		142 lbs.	26,400 mi.	157 mi.	12.7 hrs.	Sent back pictures of earth; charted "space weather."
Tiros I	U.S.A.	Apr. 1, 1960	100 years	270 lbs.	468 mi.	429 mi.	99.1 min.	Sent back 22,952 pictures of the earth's cloud cover.
Transit IB	U.S.A.	Apr. 13, 1960		265 lbs.	472 mi.	239 mi.	95.9 min.	The first navigational satellite.
Transit II and Greb	U.S.A.	June 22, 1960	50 years 50 years	265 lbs. 42 lbs.	658 mi. 658 mi.	389 mi. 389 mi.	102 min. 102 min.	First example of two satellites put into orbit by one rocket. Called "piggyback" satellite.
Echo I	U.S.A.	Aug. 12, 1960	1000 years	137.4 lbs.	1160 mi.	1018 mi.	121.6 min.	A 100-ft. communications satellite.
Courier I	U.S.A.	Oct. 4, 1960	1000 years	501 lbs.	745 mi.	500 mi.	104 min.	A communications satellite.
Sputnik VIII	U.S.S.R.	Feb. 12, 1961	13 days. Fell Feb. 25, 1961	14,300 lbs.	201.5 mi.	123 mi.	90 min.	While in orbit around earth, sent a satellite called the Venus probe into orbit around the sun.
Transit IVA, Greb, and Injun	U.S.A.	June 29, 1961	1 year		620 mi.	547 mi.	103.8 min.	Three satellites put into orbit by one rocket.
Explorer XIII	U.S.A.	Aug. 25, 1961	50 years	127 lbs.	565 mi.	275 mi.	98 min.	The 50th U.S. satellite put into orbit successfully.
Mercury-Atlas IV	U.S.A.	Sept. 13, 1961	Landed 1 hr., 49 min. after launching.	2700 lbs.	158.6 mi.	99.3 mi.	89 min.	Carried dummy simulating respiration and perspiration around earth once. Tested tracking system for manned flights.
OSO (Orbiting Solar Observatory)	U.S.A.	Mar. 8, 1962		458 lbs.	370 mi.	343 mi.	96.15 min.	Designed to solve some of the mysteries of the sun.
Telstar	U.S.A.	July 10, 1962		170 lbs.	3502 mi.	593 mi.	157.8 min.	The first international satellite for beaming television and radio programs from country to country. First privately-financed U.S. space endeavor.

OTHER SPACE PROBES

Name	Country	Date of Launching	Results
Lunik I (Metchtá)	U.S.S.R.	Jan. 2, 1959	Passed the moon and became an artificial planet traveling around the sun.
Pioneer IV	U.S.A.	Mar. 3, 1959	Passed the moon and became an artificial planet.
Lunik II	U.S.S.R.	Sept. 12, 1959	Struck the moon near the Sea of Serenity on September 13, 1959.
Lunik III	U.S.S.R.	Oct. 4, 1959	Circled the moon and sent back pictures of the far side. Went into orbit around the earth with most distant point out beyond the orbit of the moon.
Pioneer V	U.S.A.	Mar. 11, 1960	Put into orbit around sun. Sent back messages from 20,000,000 miles away.
Ranger IV	U.S.A.	April 23, 1962	Landed on far side of moon but destroyed itself and its instruments on impact.

SIX MEN IN SPACE

Lieut. Col. Yuri A. Gagarin (U.S.S.R.)
Major Gherman S. Titov (U.S.S.R.)

Lieut. Col. John H. Glenn, Jr. (U.S.A.)
Lieut. Comdr. M. Scott Carpenter (U.S.A.)

Major Andrian G. Nikolayev (U.S...
Lieut. Col. Pavel R. Popovich (U...

	GAGARIN	TITOV	GLENN	CARPENTER	NIKOLAYEV	POPOVI...
Date	4 /12 /61	8 /6 /61	2 /20 /62	5 /24 /62	8 /11 /62	8 /12 /62
Number of orbits	1	17	3	3	64	48
Altitude in miles	109—188	111—160	99—162	99—167.4	109.7—141.3	110.5—145...
Distance in miles	About 25,000	437,500	About 81,000	About 81,250	1,625,000	1,242,500
Top speed in mph	17,400	17,750	17,545	17,532	18,000	18,000
Flight time	108 min.	25 hrs., 18 min.	4 hrs., 56 min.	4 hrs., 56 min.	94 hrs., 25 min.	71 hrs., 3...
Weight of capsule	10,460 lbs.	10,430 lbs.	4,200 lbs.	4,200 lbs.	Not given	Not given
Name of capsule	Vostok I	Vostok II	Friendship 7	Aurora 7	Vostok III	Vostok IV...

LONG JOURNEYS

In 1271 Marco Polo left Venice for the court of Kublai Khan in Cathay, now called China. His 5,000-mile journey to the Far East took him over desolate deserts and high mountains and was the beginning of his famous adventures. The journey to China took about a year.

In 1492 Christopher Columbus sailed from Spain to the West Indies—a distance of about 4,000 miles—on his famous voyage of discovery. The voyage took 70 days.

In 1519 Ferdinand Magellan set out from Cadiz, Spain, to sail around the world. He died after having traveled about 20,000 miles. One of his ships, however, completed the trip 2 years and 353 days after it had set sail.

In 1960 the atomic-powered submarine "Triton" traveled under water all the way around the world, following roughly Magellan's route. The 41,519-mile trip was covered in 84 days.

The journeys made by the American and Russian astronauts are the longest trips in history. As the chart above shows, Major Nikolayev traveled 1,625,000 miles—64 times around the earth—in a little less than four days, and at a speed which reached 18,000 miles per hour. The possibility of traveling hundreds of thousands of miles in only a few days was almost unimaginable to people living even as recently as 50 years ago.

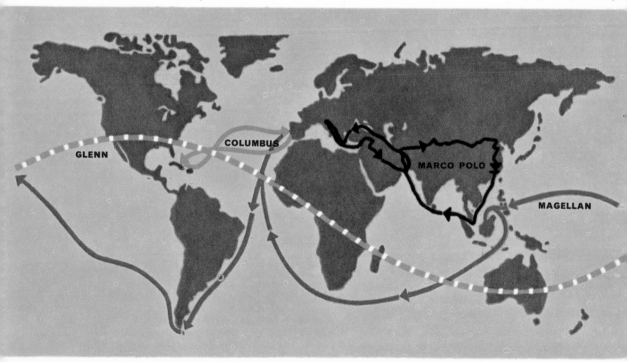

INDEX